To Whit Snyder

SEED OF VILLAINY:

THE HILTON CRAWFORD STORY

Best Wishes

Dennis Shannon

SEED OF VILLAINY:

THE HILTON CRAWFORD STORY

TANNIE SHANNON

TEXAS REVIEW PRESS
HUNTSVILLE, TEXAS

FIRST EDITION, 2007
Requests for permission to reproduce material from this work should be sent to:

Permissions
Texas Review Press
English Department
Sam Houston State University
Huntsville, TX 77341-2146

Disclaimer: All material in this book was provided by the author, who is totally responsible for all allegations, all accusations, all assumptions, all interpretations, all quoted material, and all presumed factual matter. Neither Texas Review Press nor anyone associated with the Press or Sam Houston State University may be held responsible for any material presented in this book.

Cover design by Paul Ruffin

Library of Congress Cataloging-in-Publication Data

Shannon, Tannie.
   Seed of villainy : the Hilton Crawford story / Tannie Shannon.
-- 1st ed.
      p. cm.
   ISBN-13: 978-1-881515-99-9 (pbk. : alk. paper)
   ISBN-10: 1-881515-99-0 (pbk. : alk. paper)
   1. Crawford, Hilton, 1939-2003. 2. Murderers--Texas--Montgomery
County--Case
   studies. 3. Everett, McKay, 1983-1995. 4. Murder--Texas--
Montgomery County--Case
   studies. 5. Trials (Murder)--Texas--Montgomery County--Case
studies. I. Title.
   HV6533.T4S53 2006
   364.152'3092--dc22
   [B]
                                          2006029798

I dedicate this work to my children, Chris and Laney, and their loving mother, Frances. My family is the soul of my existence, my "light in the heart."

Table of Contents

Introduction

Hilton Crawford was a friend of mine. I guess maybe that's what's so strange about this book. I thought this would be a project in which I could simply interpret the facts and reap the benefits. I learned, however, that it couldn't happen that way. When two people spend hours together—as we did, albeit through visitor's glass—sharing intimate details of their lives, I suppose a certain amount of closeness should be anticipated. But still, a man convicted of kidnapping and murdering a child that he professed to love? The mere thought of his crime angers me even now. In no way could I have imagined calling this demon a friend.

My first recollection of the name Hilton Crawford—or "Uncle Hilty," as he was called by the media—came during the investigation of McKay Everett's murder. It was the lead story in all the local newspapers, especially Conroe, where both the Everetts and I lived. I knew none of the characters involved and was no more interested in this crime than I might have been in any other local murder. That is, until our next-door neighbor Lynn Martin told my wife and me over margaritas that she had been appointed to Crawford's defense. It was three weeks before the trial was scheduled to begin. "What do I know about defending a capital murder charge? Absolutely nothing," she said between sips. "And there's so little time to prepare. I just wish the judge had picked someone else." After a short silence she added, "Tannie, you should meet this guy. He's so nice. I just don't know how he could have done this. Hell, I'd probably have trusted him with my own child."

Thus began my communication with Hilton Crawford. Lynn supplied the address and I began writing to him. One of the first questions I can remember asking was "Why?"

He wrote back and answered simply, "I don't know. That's the same question I've asked myself a million times. I wish I had the answer." I proposed that he allow me to tell his story and together we would search for the answer; he agreed. The contents of this book reveal the product of that search.

In *Seed of Villainy* I have tried to tell the story from Hilton Crawford's point of view. My sources are newspaper articles, trial transcripts, and, of course, Crawford himself. I use many hours of taped interviews, along with hundreds of personal letters. I have done my best to remain true to the events as they were told to me.

One of the controversial elements of the crime and trial is the existence of another alleged principal participant, R. L. Remington, who was never apprehended. He is included in this work as a living, breathing, culpable character. Although the F.B.I. stated after several weeks of investigation that they were unable to find Remington and it was unlikely that he existed, Crawford went to his execution (an execution that I witnessed) swearing that his story was true. For this reason, among others, I choose to believe that Crawford's version is indeed the true and accurate account of McKay Everett's abduction and murder.

—Tannie Shannon

Seed of Villainy:

The Hilton Crawford Story

We must seek the root cause of man's violence toward man—and when we find contributing factors to be the result of culture or environment we should all shoulder a portion of the blame.

This is the forest primeval. The murmuring pines and the hemlocks,
Bearded with moss, and in garments green, indistinct in the
      twilight,
Stand like Druids of eld, with voices sad and prophetic,
Stand like harpers hoar, with beards that rest on their bosoms.
Loud from its rocky caverns, the deep-voiced neighboring ocean
Speaks, and in accents disconsolate answers the wail of the forest.

"Evangeline," Henry Wadsworth Longfellow

Part 1: Fleeing the Scene

I

The Chrysler sat motionless and silent. Its lone occupant stared blankly into the black Louisiana night. There had been no need to pull to the side of the road. Seldom used in daylight hours, at 2 a.m. it was completely deserted. It was as if the vehicle had been swallowed into the bowels of the Atchafalaya swamp. There the driver sat, waiting for reason—logic—to lead him back into the world of the living.

There were sounds, of course, swamp noise, insects mostly. Their hum and chirp rose in a cadence that swelled and subsided in a rhythm that seemed to mimic the restless murmur of a sleeping leviathan. Yet, to the driver, the swamp was mute. If the spirit of Evangeline herself had chosen that moment to tap-dance on the car's hood, he would not have noticed. He was lost, not in the swamp's mossy confines, but in an even more complex maze: Hilton Crawford was trapped in the tangled jungle of his own mind.

He sat like a stone, while inside emotion flowed like an enraged river. Unable to move, he waited as the feelings surged. Anger, disgust, guilt, fear—all rolled and boiled through his body until they found a murky confluence in his gut.

His immediate problem was regaining the ability to think. Thoughts came not in complete logical sequences but in abstract segments. He tried to concentrate, tried to force his brain to respond by telling him what to do next, but each time he posed a logical question, a rush of anger or remorse would interfere, jetties deflecting the flow of logic. Crawford never used drugs, but later he would compare the sensations of this night to what he envisioned as a bad acid trip. Recalling the stories of some of the druggies he had arrested back in the seventies, they seemed very similar.

In darkness he sat, stoned on guilt, as he relived the horror of what he had witnessed this night. Memories came in fragments. He had been lied to, manipulated, and worse, he had been weak—a coward. It wasn't him, couldn't be. He was neither weak nor easily intimidated. He had served his country as a Marine. He'd been a respected police officer for many years. He was, in fact, twice Officer of the Year. Who would remember now? He wasn't a bad man. Always tried to do the right thing. Hadn't he always given Connie everything she wanted? He was a good provider, taught his boys right from wrong. They were good boys. What would they think? What about all the kids he had helped? Hell, he coached little league ball for twenty years—no, check that, *thirty* years. He gave his own time and money, lots of money. Whenever the team needed something, or even one of the players for that matter, he dug into his own pocket and came up with it. He bought equipment, paid for uniforms, even after his own sons were too old to play. What would all those kids think? And the teachers, the ones who worked with Connie. They always liked him. Didn't he take them on trips? Took them and their husbands to Vegas. Even the Everetts—took Paulette's husband, that son-of-a-bitch Carl. Who would remember any of that now?

Crawford was working through the guilt. Thoughts were still fragmented, but at least they were beginning to make sense. He knew he wasn't a bad guy, not really. It was Carl's fault. If the greedy prick hadn't fucked him on the oil deal, or if he had just apologized. He never said shit, just took advantage of the friendship and then forgot about it. Crawford didn't forget, though. It wasn't the money, just ten thousand dollars, it was the principle. The principle and the lack of respect. And later, when Carl started doing so good in that Amway business, he just kept rubbing his nose in it. If he hadn't done all that, that bragging, saying he had five hundred thousand in one account and seven-fifty in another. Well, if he hadn't done that . . . .

In a start Crawford reached for the ignition and brought the Chrysler to life. The movement, almost involuntary, and the car's shudder, affected him like brushing a high-voltage wire. Both hands shot upward. "Fuck it," he screamed. "Fuck it! Fuck them! Fuck me!" His right fist slammed hard into the dash. Pain was strangely comforting. He brought the bruised knuckles to his lips and wiped away the mucus. Then he cried.

II

Hilton Crawford, or Buddy, as his friends knew him until he was in his twenties, didn't seem the criminal type. There was no childhood trauma, there were no abusive parents or siblings, no pedophilic episodes with a trusted friend, nothing to which psychologists could point and say, "There. That is the reason. That is what caused his aberrant behavior. That is the reason he committed such a vile act." By all accounts, Hilton Crawford lived an idyllic American childhood.

Estelle Crawford pushed open the screen door. "Buddy, it's time to come in," she called. She called to Hilton Jr. by the pet name his sister had given him years earlier. "You boys can come back tomorrow and play again."

Her request went unanswered. Eddie Warren had taken the rebound and, falling backward, lobbed a desperation shot that glanced off the backboard and fell through the basket. Buddy grabbed the ball, cradling it under his left arm as he extended his right hand to help his fallen friend.

"I said it's time to come in, dear."

"Okay, Mom—in a minute."

Buddy took the ball past the imaginary center-court line. It was a two-on-one competition and his opponents had just scored. He turned suddenly, catching one of his opponents off guard. It was all the edge he needed—he sidestepped and drove the basket. He judged the distance and leaped. He was probably no more than six inches off the ground, but in his mind his feet were springs. He released the ball in mid-flight. From instinct, he knew the shot was good.

His father's voice rang above the raucous chatter: "Son, your mother said it was time to come in."

Hilton Senior exuded a patriarchal strength common for the era. He was protector and provider. Nothing—no hardship—could touch his family. It was this quality that earned him the respect of others, his friends and family. Buddy idolized his father. Without protest, he said goodnight to his friends.

III

It was between three and four in the morning when Crawford crossed the Sabine River and I-10 began to look more like a freeway again. Behind him, the road was a straight shot from the Texas border all the way to New Orleans, if one cared to go that far. It was almost like its planners had used a ruler. Just dropped it on a map, drew a line and said here—here is where we'll build the road. Hardly a curve anywhere. They even built it straight across the swamp, just raised it up some. Starting about six miles east of Lafayette, the road becomes something like a long, very long, bridge. You can drive for miles, as much as twenty miles at a stretch, without an exit. Crawford had never driven that road without wondering about the engineering. How the hell did they do it? Maybe barges, huge barges, capable of floating the enormous concrete pillars that supported the road. No matter. He did know one thing for sure, though—it's best to stop and piss in Lafayette if you're going east.

One of the few exits was Whiskey Bay, the place he had just left. It was nothing, nowhere, just a place in the swamp, maybe a little higher than the rest. There was no town or settlement there, not a living person that he knew of. There was a sign that said something about a wildlife management area. It was on the road he had driven down, the only road there, hardly more than ruts hewn out of the swamp. It was trashy, not like home, not like Texas. He had glimpsed abandoned tires and appliances, things people tired of and wanted to forget. Now there was a body there, and that was something Crawford wanted desperately to forget.

IV

The basketball goal was already there when seven-year-old Hilton Crawford came to live in the modest frame house on Zavalla. With the help of Jack Martin, then coach at Lamar University, Hilton Senior made certain it was built correctly, laid out to proper measurements. Buddy's father left nothing to chance. Where family was concerned, influence and guidance of his children, he was especially tenacious. He insisted that the court and goal were set to regulation.

Buddy paid little notice of the house his father had painstakingly built with his own hands. It was just a place to come to after school: to eat, to play, to feel love and comfort, to be seven years old. But his backyard was another matter. Even while his parents and older sister were moving their belongings into the new home, he lobbed shots toward a goal that was out of reach, too high for a seven-year-old.

The lawn was carpeted with a thick layer of hardy St. Augustine, but no grass could long contend with the frequent footfalls of eager young athletes. Before Buddy's twelfth year the grass had disappeared. In its place was barren earth, packed hard as cement by the force of pounding feet and bouncing balls.

The yard was a neighborhood meeting place for boys. Often, twenty or more would gather. The pecking order changed from year to year, as faces and bodies changed, but Buddy always stayed close to the top. He excelled, not because of his superior size or athletic ability, but by sheer determination. Crawford's obsessive nature gave him the magic ingredient needed to win consistently, something coaches call heart.

Buddy learned that quitting was not acceptable. *Quit* was synonymous with *lose,* and no one respected a loser. Injuries, pain, size, and inability were only challenges to be overcome. Life itself was a game in which success meant winning, and self-worth was measured in success. Grass would never be able to grow on Crawford's playing field.

He was a happy child. Both parents supported and encouraged his competitive nature. On sweltering Texas afternoons Estelle made lemonade—not the kind made from mix or concentrate, but the good stuff, made by squeezing the juice from dozens of lemons and heaping in pure white sugar till sweet overpowered sour. The boys drank the sticky-sweet liquid in huge gulps, anxiously tilting faster than their mouths and throats could work, while the excess spilled onto sweat-drenched stomachs. Glasses emptied, and they played on, oblivious to the Texas heat, focused only on the game.

V

At last he was back in Texas, in Beaumont. Back home. Not where he had lived for the last thirty or so years, but where he was raised—where he still felt he belonged. There was a comfort in being there, like the feel of a mother's embrace. He wished his mother was still alive so he could go to her now. He wanted to lay his head on her aproned lap and feel the comfort of her voice as she told him everything would be okay. "Shhh, hush now," she would say. "Whatever you've done, it'll be all right. God will forgive you. God loves you." He wanted to hear the words so badly that he said them aloud, or maybe he only thought he said them. Hell, he wished he could go back, back all the way to the womb. No light, no sound, no guilt, no anger, only peace. Comfort!

"I said, can I help you, sir?" The clerk raised her voice slightly. No one else was present in the lobby of the Best Western.

"Uh, um, Crawford," he said.

"Yes sir, Mr. Crawford." Her fingers tapped rapidly at the keyboard. "Would you prefer a king or two full-size?"

"Um, whatever, don't matter."

"Very well, sir. Fill out the top portion—and I'll need your credit card."

Crawford fumbled with the billfold. He retrieved it topside down and the loose contents, mostly scraps of paper and business cards, fell, scattered at his feet. He bent and fumbled with the contents. First he chose a Visa card with the name Kevin Crawford. But, reconsidering, he sorted through the pile to find the only card in his own name, an American Express, and placed it in front of the clerk. Then he stooped to recover the remaining items.

It was in this position in the well-lighted lobby that he first noticed the blood—tiny spatters covering the front of his shirt. How? Then he recalled. He was running toward them. He was close when the first shot was fired. He had heard the explosion and seen the length of fire from the end of the gun, the flash that erupted through and past the boy's head. He felt the blast, the rush of air, the slight sting of residue—at least, he thought it was residue—from the gunpowder. He was facing them, very close. He felt it on the front of his clothing and on his face. Shit! There must be blood on his face. He had turned away as the second shot was fired. There might even be blood on his back.

He rose slowly, turned sideways to the clerk. She was busy with the registration, never even looked at him. It was past four in the morning. Who looks at faces at that time of day?

"We are here," she said and plotted the room's location on a motel diagram.

He thanked her and left with head bowed, like the suspects he questioned when he was a captain in the Sheriff's Department. That was fifteen years ago, or maybe twenty—when he was well respected. Who would remember after tonight?

VI

Buddy (Hilton), excelled at all sports from a very young age. Basketball and baseball were his favorite games, but he was good at football and track too. He tried singing as well, and joined the church choir. In spite of the fact that his voice was admittedly imperfect—"couldn't sing a lick"—in his words, he continued the activity for two years. During his mid-teen years, ages fourteen to sixteen, most of his Saturday nights were occupied with either practice or city-wide competition among choir groups. While other teenagers were going to see Brando's anguished screaming for Stella in *A Streetcar Named Desire* or movies in which aliens penetrate the spinal cords of humans and control their actions, Buddy was belting out "The Old Rugged Cross" and "Just a Closer Walk." The songs made him feel good, but the real reason he did it was for approval. *That Buddy Crawford is such a good boy—a gifted athlete and he does so love the Lord.*

As to girls, he was shy and awkward, preferring athletic competition to female company. He didn't meet his first real love until his junior year in high school. It was during a basketball game between

South Park High and Vidor—a grudge match. The proximity of the two schools fostered a rivalry that always resulted in intense competition. In spite of the fact that he was a key player, it was during this contest that Buddy first noticed Barbara May. She sat midway in the stands.

The on-court action was fast-paced, the kind of game that usually requires focus. In this kind of struggle there are no faces, only noise and motion and bodies. It was unlikely that he should have seen her at all. One glance was all it took, one moment of eye contact, a brief smile. Then, after each play, at every opportunity, he looked for her. And she was there, returning his gaze. Yet, in spite of the distraction, or maybe because of it, Buddy managed to score nineteen points. He became the star of the game.

The following day, Cecille Perkins, a mutual friend, stopped Buddy between classes. "I know someone who thinks you're really cute."

Buddy tried to seem indifferent. "Oh yeah, and who would that be?"

Cecille blurted, "Barbara—Barbara May." She was oblivious to his feigned lack of interest. "She thinks you are sooo cool. She goes to all the ballgames just to watch you play." Cecille spoke so fast that Buddy could hardly understand her.

"How bout that? Thanks for the info. I think she's cute too."

Cecille disappeared into the milling throng of students. She had gotten the reply she wanted—it was time to relay his mutual interest.

Barbara May's looks and personality combined to make her one of the most popular girls in school. She had a quality that allowed her to seem both friendly and aloof at the same time. While it endeared her to fellow students, it made her appear almost untouchable to would-be boyfriends. For this reason, Buddy had never considered asking her out. But after the eye contact during the Vidor game, and Cecille's reinforcement, he was ready.

South Park's cafeteria was loud with the clatter of cooking pans and teenagers as Buddy shoved his tray along. Women in white aprons and tightened hairnets filled it with portions appropriate for the student's size and gender. At 6' 1" Buddy got generous servings. He nodded to the meatloaf with tomato sauce, a better choice than the sauerkraut and wieners. A woman with flabby arms ladled it onto the tray. The flesh above her elbows shook like Jell-O with each movement, and he wondered what it would be like to touch. After the meatloaf came mashed potatoes, limp and plain, and peas. Finally, bread pudding with raisins. Bread pudding was served frequently, and he wondered if maybe it wasn't just a way to use all the leftover bread. He balanced a pair of milk cartons on the tray's edge while he fished the weekly meal ticket from his shirt pocket. The routine had been long established. Buddy's father insisted that he eat lunch in the cafeteria—any diet approved by the United States government and implemented by the school system had to be healthy.

Buddy scanned the room. He found Barbara sitting with three other girls and asked to join them. With a self-confidence that left him off guard, she answered, "Sure—sit here, Buddy." She slid down the bench, allowing room beside her. The other girls restrained themselves, swallowing their urges to giggle.

"Uh—you think I'm cute?"

She smiled, and replied gracefully, "Yes, Buddy, I think you're very nice." Then she added, "And such a smooth talker." Her friends could no longer contain themselves—they laughed openly.

Buddy felt he was the object of their humor, but he couldn't figure out the joke. Just the silliness of girls, he reasoned. "So—you want to go to the drive-in Saturday?"

It didn't matter what was playing or who was starring—young couples didn't go to the drive-in to watch movies. The idea was to be alone, where they could talk, and kiss if they wanted, or simply get to know each other without adult supervision.

"Sure, I'd love to. But, come over a little early, maybe around six. You'll have to meet my parents."

Barbara knew that her father would be pleased with Buddy. His clean-cut, athletic appearance and his polite manner made him seem like the perfect all-American kid. Buddy was a trophy, and she wanted to show him off.

Just as she had thought, Buddy and her father liked each other instantly. The movie started at dusk, but by then they were so engrossed in sports talk that Barbara had to twice remind Buddy it was time to go.

"I like your folks," he remarked after they were on their way. "Especially your dad. He says he might have a job for me this summer."

Barbara smiled.

That night Buddy and Barbara enjoyed the first of what became a weekly ritual, Saturday nights at the South Park drive-in. In the darkness, by the theater's rearmost speakers, they experimented with passion: electric kisses, touches and words—declarations, promises, pledges.

Buddy and Barbara were sweethearts for the remainder of their high school years. They were together constantly. He drove her to school in the '51 Ford given him by his father when the family purchased a newer model. They walked to class and ate lunch together. She wore his letter jacket and senior ring. After high school, however, their relationship began to fade.

Buddy had taken a job with Barbara's father during the summer of his junior year and continued to work after graduation, frequently traveling out of state. As a bead welder he earned as much as $9.00 an hour, a salary envied by many adults in 1958. But following pipeline construction was not to Buddy's liking. It depressed him to be away from friends and family for months at a time. And life without competition or challenge was boring to him. He returned home and did what he thought was next expected of him: He enlisted in the Marine Corps Reserve.

VII

Crawford thought his luck might be changing after getting by the desk clerk. The slight comfort disappeared when he left the motel office and found more incriminating evidence. The rear bumper and trunk lid were smeared with blood. The point of surprise was now past. He recalled the dull thuds from the back of the car. That was when he should have stopped it! At least tried. The boy might still be alive. But, shit! What could he have done? Just caused trouble for everybody. He thought it best to just let it play out and see what happened. He didn't know it would go that far, though. As he looked inside the trunk, vivid recollections of the Whiskey Bay scene came to him.

Shit! All that blood!

He reacted instinctively. Crawford was a survivor. The most important thing was to get rid of the evidence. He located his room and parked in the darkness at the back of the lot. Using wet towels and a little bar of hand soap from the room, he scrubbed. The blood outside the car, the bumper and trunk lid, cleaned up nicely. Even in dim light he could tell the car's exterior was clean. He was relieved. It was good he had noticed it before daylight.

Inside the trunk was different. He expected to see a lot of blood, but not that much. Shit! What happened back here? Did he cut an artery or something? Stuff was covered, like it had come out in spurts.

There were three gym bags. One was full of golf balls, new ones, still in the boxes. Another contained underwear, jockey shorts, a dozen or so, brand new, still packaged. A third was full of papers: correspondence, unused business forms, payroll sheets—things that usually accumulate in a bottom desk drawer. The bags were covered with blood, but the contents seemed fine. He put the bags in the motel dumpster, pushed them down deep where no one would notice. He didn't know what to do with the rest. He dumped everything into the back seat. He would figure out later whether or not to keep it. There was also a gun, the gun that had been used to kill McKay, which he was sure he would keep and hide somewhere. It was a nice gun, a Smith and Wesson .45 automatic.

He blotted and scrubbed, wringing out towels and starting again. He brought water from his room in a plastic trashcan so he could rinse the towels. He would wipe blood from the carpet in one spot, and then start on another. Five minutes later the spot he had just cleaned would appear again. He was tired. Before, he had functioned on adrenaline rush, fatigue masked with fear, but busywork quenched the adrenaline. He wanted sleep, to rest, but knew he couldn't stop. He continued to scrub. Bloodstains didn't come out easily, but they shouldn't be that hard to remove. At daybreak he stopped. He couldn't very well stand there mopping blood out of his trunk while people passed on their way to work.

VIII

It was past midnight when the busses carrying Buddy and the other Marine recruits arrived at the company area designated for their basic training.

"Line up, you shitheads!"

"Dress right! Dress right!"

Sleepy-eyed boys shuffled into positions indicated by cadre. They moved awkwardly, looking both right and left in the futile hope that they stood next to someone who comprehended the order—someone they could mimic. They stumbled and bumped and tripped and allowed the angry voices to wash over them. A half-dozen men, mixed noncoms—corporals and sergeants, they would later learn—poked and prodded them into position.

Adding to their insecurity were incredibly bright lights that all seemed to point in their direction. The recruits squinted toward the source of the voice. He was on a raised platform, framed before the floodlights. They weren't able to see his face—the direction and intensity of the lighting shadowed his features to such an extent that he was visible only as a silhouette. But they saw the rigidity of his frame, more statue than man.

Almost bigger than life, he stood with feet firmly planted eighteen inches apart. Left arm folded behind his back, his right hand held the microphone locked in position just below his chin. The triangular hat with its wide brim further blocking the light topped the black space where his face should have been.

"I am Gunnery Sergeant Stinson. You are now in my charge. I am a non-commissioned officer." He spoke as stiffly as he stood—no contractions, emphasis on every word. "You do not call me *sir*. You will address me as *sergeant*. When I ask you a question you will answer with *yes, sergeant* or *no, sergeant*. Is that clear?"

Some nervous shifting. A few answered yes.

"Is—that—*clear*?" The voice was even louder, more threatening.

"Yes—*sergeant*." The reply was louder and more in unison.

"I—can't—*hear*—you!"

"*Yes, sergeant*!" No hesitation. All spoke as one.

"Good. Now that you know who I am, let me tell you who you are. You are maggots! You are slimy worms! You are not Marines! We will teach you how to *become* Marines! You are also not motherfuckers! And you are not cocksuckers! I do not like these words, and anyone who uses them will deal with me personally! Is that *clear*?"

"*Yes, sergeant*!"

"Good. Now I am going to leave you in the capable hands of Corporal Kowalski. He will call roll, after which you will be dismissed to your assigned barracks. Reveille is at 0400 hours. Get a good night's sleep. You'll need it tomorrow."

Crawford looked at his watch. It was already 1 a.m. How would anyone get a good night's sleep?

It was still dark when he was startled awake. In the midst of noise and clatter and urgency, Crawford realized that it was time to get up. His platoon sergeant had just kicked his bunk, hard enough to move it six inches or more on the tile floor.

"Ten minutes—you've got ten minutes!" Staff Sergeant DeWolfe, in charge of Crawford's platoon, was weaving his way through the disarray of footlockers and scattered clothing left over from the previous night. He ordered, urged, cursed, and shoved men into action.

DeWolfe was one of the more brutal platoon sergeants in Crawford's company. Rumor had it that he was twice busted in rank for assaulting trainees. He was a career soldier and a veteran of the Korean conflict. He was said to have been involved in the battle of Pusan, one of only a dozen survivors left in an entire company. He had a way of thrusting his face toward you in an aggressive posture, while yelling obscenities with little perceptible lip movement—they seemed to remain a constant half-inch apart. Adding to the picture was a misshapen growth at the bottom of his face, making it always look like he was drooling, like saliva was dripping from his chin.

"Outside! Outside! Move it! Move it! Les go! Les go! Move it! Move it! Move it!" DeWolfe stood in the doorway, waving his arms and giving each recruit that passed a push that propelled the young soldier forward and down the barrack steps. Many of them first found Bravo company soil with their knees and palms.

During the second week of basic, several of the better-conditioned recruits, including Buddy, decided they would show the sergeant up. They taunted him into an endurance run. Buddy was one of the last two standing, but they never came close to matching DeWolfe's stamina.

"Lemme know when you ladies are ready to quit." DeWolfe ran some of the last few miles backwards—grinning at them above the distorted growth on his chin.

The scenario became routine. DeWolfe's rule was always urgent and forever absolute. His trainees were never capable, never fast enough, never neat enough. But Crawford learned quickly. He learned to be first out the door. He accepted the regimen as he had accepted the didactic rule of his high school coaches. DeWolfe may not have been capable of outright approval, but Crawford was surely one of his favorites.

Crawford's athletic training and discipline had been the perfect precursor for Marine boot camp. While some had trouble adapting, Crawford's military experience was pleasant, even fun. The rigorous physical activity agreed with him. He entered in good shape, but the six months he spent on active duty served to transform both body and being. His manner matured to one of manly pride and silent dignity.

IX

Sleep. There comes a time when life-sustaining needs—hunger and sleep—displace emotions, even the strongest, even fear. It was time to rest. He opened another bar of motel soap and washed his hands and face. He watched the bloody water flow in circlets and disappear. And his hands were clean. There were still spatters on his clothing, but there was nothing he could do about that. He had done what he could and it was time to sleep.

He lay face up, fully clothed. He fought the memory, the guilt, desperation that smothers you as if you were buried alive. He forced his mind to more pleasant thoughts. He remembered his wedding. The church was only a few blocks from where he now lay. It was magnificent, and more than six hundred people attended. They came to honor him and his bride, Connie. He saw her through a window of his mind as she walked toward him in her beautiful fully-veiled dress. What a vision she was.

He panned the room. The faces were different, not right. There were no more happy wedding-faces, no smiles, no happy tears. Looks were harsh and disapproving. As he watched, the faces became more distorted, angry. Men pointed at him, then swore and shook their fists. Women screamed and cried and began to throw things at him, horrible things—excrement. It stuck to him, his clothing, his face! He looked back at Connie. She still walked toward him, through the clamor. Then she lifted her veil. Her face wasn't like the rest, not angry, not distorted. It was worse. In her face he saw disgust—and pity. And she began to shake her head.

He woke, startled. It was still early. He had slept only a few minutes, but it was long enough. There was still much to do. First, though, he would call Connie. He needed her support.

Crawford expected to hear a sleepy hello after several rings. He was surprised when Connie answered immediately. She was agitated. He heard no drawn-out, barely audible greeting usually received at this hour. Instead came a loud, urgent hello, followed by news of McKay Everett's kidnapping.

"Hilton, Carl's been trying to contact you," she said. "He thinks that with your background as a police officer you may be able to help them—you know, with advice, or contacts—or whatever. He called late last night, very upset. I didn't know what to say, I just told him we'd try and help, if we could. Then I called their neighbor, Nancy—um—Nancy Kahn, and the Schaeffers, just to see if they'd heard anything. They think Elizabeth may have been on the phone with McKay when he was taken. They're scared, Hilton. So am I. I wish you were home."

Crawford hesitated. He wanted to unburden himself, just blurt out the whole sorry mess. Connie would forgive him. She would be hurt, would cry a lot. But she'd know he couldn't have meant for this to happen, not like this. Then he remembered the dream, the look of disgust as she lifted her veil, the revulsion underneath.

"I'll be there as soon as I can," he said. "I'll do whatever I can for Carl. You know that. I'll try to get hold of him later on. It's hard to predict how these things will turn out. Maybe everything will be all right—I hope so. For now, though, I think I oughta call that Kahn woman and find out what's happening."

Connie read off the phone number for Nancy Kahn. The urgency in her voice reinforced Crawford's decision to remain silent about his involvement. "Hilton, hurry home, please. I need you here. I love you."

"I—I love you too. I'll be home as soon as I can, just a few more things to take care of here."

Crawford replaced the receiver and sat stiffly on the edge of the bed. He had spoken to Connie, but it wasn't the conversation he wanted to have. The news about Carl Everett calling his home was unexpected, caught him off guard. He needed to talk to someone about the kidnapping, find out what they knew. He couldn't face talking to Carl, though. Not yet. He paced, vacillating. Finally, he sighed deeply and dialed the number for Nancy Kahn.

"Hello?" she answered. It sounded more like a question than an answer.

"Hello, Nancy, uh, Mrs. Kahn?"

"Yes, this is Nancy Kahn."

"This is Hilton Crawford. You talked with my wife last night, about McKay."

"Oh, hello, Hilton. We're all just worried sick. I'm sure you've heard all about it, his being taken last night, kidnapped and all. Anyway, Carl was trying to find you to see if you could come over and help. I mean, he knows you were a policeman and thought you might have some contacts, know somebody that might help."

"Yeah, I heard. Connie was just telling me about it. It's terrible. Please tell the Everetts how sorry I am. I'm out of town, but as soon as I heard the news I made arrangements to finish up here and come home. I'll be back this afternoon. Tell Carl I'll be glad to help in any way I can. Do they have any leads yet?" He didn't have to feign concern with the last question.

"Well, I think there are some leads," she said. "You know, of course, the FBI's been called in."

Crawford chilled. He expected that, just not this soon.

"Bill, my husband, thinks he may have seen them last night—the kidnappers. He was puttin' out the garbage and a car backed out of their driveway real fast. It almost hit him."

"Did he get the license number?" He tried to control the tension in his voice.

"No. It didn't occur to him. He didn't know anything was wrong. He just thought it was a careless driver or something. It, well, it made him mad, but there wasn't anything he could do about it. Anyway, it was big, maybe a Chrysler. He thinks maybe it was green, could have been some other color, though. But he did notice one thing for sure. It had a dealer's emblem on the trunk, shaped like a crown."

Crawford's spirit sank. He thanked her and hung up the phone.

Damn! He thought. Who could have known that asshole would be taking out the trash? At least he didn't get the license number. The Crown emblem would have to be removed, though, before anyone noticed. It was a good thing he called her. Maybe things would work out after all.

X

When Buddy returned from the required six months of active duty, his father's attitude toward him seemed to change. Hilton Sr.'s pride was obvious as he watched his son, standing straight and tall, smartly dressed in his uniform, with its polished brass and highly glossed low-quarter shoes. During basic training the younger Crawford's posture had improved dramatically. No longer did his shoulders slump while he sat, and when he stood, his spine appeared to have no curvature. His father once remarked that it looked like there was a board under his shirt. His gait had also changed. No longer did he take long, gangly strides, his head dipping and bobbing. Now his steps were sharp and crisp, and there was purpose to his movement. The elder Crawford now seemed unable to tire of his son's company. The family frequently went out to dinner, something they hadn't done before Buddy's return. Then, they, father and son, would shoot hoops in their backyard or sit talking, long after the rest of the family was sleeping soundly.

There were newspaper articles, clipped from the Beaumont Enterprise and pasted into the scrapbook his mother had kept since his junior high school years. Copies of stories, telling of his enlistment and subsequent graduations from basic and advanced training, had been sent to Buddy in San Diego. During off hours he had read the articles and imagined the people back home were reading them also. He envisioned their pride. Secretly, he wanted to fight in a war and win a medal, with the presentation to be made in his hometown. He saw a great crowd of people, all dressed in their Sunday best, each trying for a better look at their hero. There was a band, of course. It played the National Anthem, and everyone yelled and cheered for him, just like at the ballgames. It was a fantasy replayed many times.

Although he had managed to sleep only a short while, maybe fifteen minutes or less, Crawford was awake and alert. The adrenaline had returned, and he knew there was much left to do. While still early morning, Crawford left the Best Western and went north, toward the area known as Big Thicket. There was still a mess inside the trunk. That was a problem to be solved before he could return to Conroe.

It took three attempts on the cellular to locate Billy Allen. He could depend on Billy. Their friendship spanned several years and had fostered an occasional business deal, the shady kind, the kind that required mutual trust. That morning Billy was at his storage rental business in Lumberton, only a few miles north of Beaumont. It would be a good place to talk, better than going to his home.

Crawford had to now decide how much, or how little, he should tell his friend. He couldn't tell the truth, everything that had happened. No one, not even Billy, would understand. The truth was something he could never tell anyone. Well, maybe Connie, eventually, not for a long time, though. For now, he would make something up. It didn't have to be foolproof, Billy would understand. Even if he didn't believe it, he would accept it. On the way, Crawford stopped and bought a bottle of champagne. Friendship like Billy's should always be acknowledged.

Crawford saw his friend standing beside a fifty-five-gallon drum used to burn trash. It was already coughing out clouds of dense gray smoke. He was holding, sort of leaning, on a shovel, enjoying what was probably a pleasant, early-morning conversation with Gary Capo, another longtime friend of Crawford's. However, in spite of the fact that he had known Capo even longer than Billy, he could not bring himself to acknowledge the man's presence. He approached the pair and shook hands, still without looking directly into Capo's face. Later he would not even be able to recall the presence of Capo, so intense was his emotional state.

"I've got some business to discuss," said Crawford. His statement was vague, disjointed, like he was talking to no one in particular.

Capo sensed there was something the two men needed to discuss privately. He excused himself, told Crawford it was good to see him and to stay in touch, and he left them to resolve their unknown dilemma.

Allen knew Crawford well, knew his moods. It wasn't hard to know there was a problem. "What's on your mind, Buddy?"

"I need a favor. I have a few things I need to store for a while."

"Sure, I got some of my own stuff in that unit." Allen pointed to the one he had in mind. The door was already open. "Put whatever you want in there. There's plenty of room. Anything else you need?"

"Yeah, there is. I've sort of—well—gotten myself in a little jam. I'm hopin' you can help me out." The words were cumbersome, hard to deliver.

There was nothing tentative in Allen's response. "That's what friends are for. Let's hear it."

Crawford was relieved, but not surprised. "I've done a very stupid thing," he said, beginning his story with the only truth it would contain. "I put a new guard on duty that didn't have a license. I know I shouldn't have, but I was shorthanded. I needed somebody right away. Anyhow, this guy had a shootout last night and got hit in the arm."

"Damn! Is he okay?"

"Yeah, well, it's not too serious. Actually, the bullet just grazed him. It wasn't even bad enough to go to the doctor. But, the thing is, if anybody finds out what happened, I could lose my permit. I need to make sure that doesn't happen."

"All right, how can I help?"

"Well, I loaned him a pistol to use until he could afford to buy one, the same gun he used in the shooting. Maybe you could keep it for me—in case something comes up. I don't think he hit anyone, but he might have."

"No problem. Anything else?"

"Yeah, I made this guy ride in the trunk while I was taking him to his parent's house, so he wouldn't get blood inside my car. But he was bleeding more than I thought, and now I need to clean out my trunk." Crawford realized how ridiculous the story sounded as he heard it aloud. But he knew Allen wouldn't ask any questions.

Allen agreed to help remove the stains and they purchased a bottle of cleaner from a nearby Wal-Mart. They opened the trunk, wearing the somber expressions of triage nurses about to inspect an open wound. Allen reached down and touched the liner. It was almost dry, but a little of the residue came off on his fingers.

"Doesn't look too bad," he said.

Crawford had already begun to transfer the saved items from the trunk's contents into a green garbage bag. Everything that was left he had decided to keep, the rest had gone into the motel dumpster. The golf balls, the underwear, miscellaneous papers, and, most notably, the gun—all went into the green bag. The bag, in turn, went into Allen's storage room. Then, with the help of 409 All-Purpose Cleaner they began to clean, to wipe away the bloody stains.

The cleaning attempt lasted well into the morning. Crawford worked diligently, soaking the liner with cleaning solution and scrubbing with a stiff-bristled brush, then rinsing and blotting. Still, the faint rusty-pink color of blood appeared when rubbed with a dry cloth. Finally, he declared the liner a lost cause.

"Got a screwdriver I can borrow?" he called to Allen, who had resumed his storage lot duties.

After finding a screwdriver of the proper size and type in the toolbox of Allen's truck, Crawford started to loosen the tiny black screws that held the plastic pop-rivets in place. As he worked, he began to realize that pulling out the liner was the best plan. He would buy a matching liner from a wrecking yard and replace it. Then there would be no risk of a police lab finding bloodstains or any telltale hairs or fibers. He began to regain a little composure. Once more, he felt like things might work out.

"Just lift and pull," he said, speaking only to himself. The plastic fasteners popped like dozens of bottles of champagne being opened at once. He dragged the liner to an open storage room and returned to inspect the trunk's interior. It had the clean look of bare metal. It would be nice if the human brain had a liner that could be so easily pulled off, stripped away and discarded, along with all the ugliness embedded in its memory.

He exhaled and shut the lid. "Billy, you don't know how much I appreciate this. Let me know if you need something—I'll repay the favor."

Allen smiled. He took the hand that was offered. "Anytime," he said. "That's what friends are for."

"I almost forgot," said Crawford. From the Chrysler's rear floorboard he brought the bottle of champagne. He presented it as a gift for Allen's wife. It was wrapped in a white motel towel. "Here, give this to Diane."

With a final slap to Allen's shoulder Crawford left the storage lot. In the rear-view mirror he could see his friend return to the burn barrel. It was good to have true friends, ones you could count on.

He felt more comfortable. He had thanked his friend properly, now he could return to Conroe and deal with the rest. On the way he would call Nancy Kahn again. He needed to know if there would be any more surprises waiting for him, things he hadn't figured on. Already he knew something had to be done about his clothes, the blood spatters. He would be sure to have them cleaned.

Again he tried to focus on remembering any details he may have missed. It was like a big chalkboard: just erase and the problem disappears.

Erase . . . .

XII

After the Marines came Panola Junior College in Carthage, 160 miles from Beaumont—two boring semesters. Crawford had a full athletic scholarship, but he wasn't well-known. No one cheered for him. He was just a team member. And the junior college crowd didn't seem to take sports seriously. They never had good turnouts. Maybe it would have been different if he had chosen a larger school.

Besides, he had met the love of his life, Connie Parigi, and she was back in Beaumont. Crawford was smitten. They dated regularly, whenever he came home, but it wasn't often enough. Crawford decided to leave Panola College for Lamar University in Beaumont and become a police officer. He could stay at home where he would be close to Connie, and where people knew his name.

Crawford separated the pants and shirt and smoothed them out carefully on the bed. He still lived in his parents' house, but only for convenience sake. He was no longer a child. Yet, in the privacy of his own room, he knew that putting on the clothes and the badge represented a passage. He felt as if the garments would validate his manhood—dressing in official blue would afford him the rights of other men, all men, including those he most respected. At the top of that list was his father.

He looked at his reflection in the full-length mirror attached to the bathroom door. He looked good. The uniform was pressed and smooth, its crisp creases firm testament to former military training—professional pride. Even his mother, in spite of her apprehension for the job, commented on how nice he looked.

"My!" The word was exhaled rather than voiced. "Don't you look handsome!" Crawford knew she had wanted to say more. Her pride did not outweigh her worry. She turned and closed the door. Mrs. Crawford had long since learned that women should not question the choices of men they loved. She offered what encouragement she could and did her best to hide the tears.

His father, on the other hand, was overjoyed. Of course, the elder Hilton Crawford would have been supportive of his son, no matter what his occupation. But to be a police officer was perfect. Devotion to public service, and Buddy would be someone respected, someone everyone would look up to. It was exactly what Hilton Crawford Senior would have envisioned for his son, a profession a man could take pride in.

Part 2: The Investigation and Arrest

I

Anthony Wargo, special agent with the Conroe Division of the FBI, arrived at the Everett house around 1:30 a.m. on Wednesday morning. He was responding to a call from the Houston office. A suspected kidnapping had occurred. Little was known other than that a child was missing and a ransom call had been received. Wargo was responsible for operations at the scene—conducting interviews and the like. Under the direction of Bill Jones, senior agent in charge of the case, he was to coordinate efforts with other investigators, some of whom were already there.

Wargo graduated from Ohio State University in 1982 with a degree in accounting. But analyzing crime scenes and catching bad guys seemed like a more interesting profession. Thus, rather than fill his days by filing tax extensions for wealthy clients, he joined the FBI. He completed the Bureau's academy at Quantico and was assigned to the Houston Division. His entire career, other than a couple of years in Chicago, had been spent in the area; the last four years he was in the bureau's Conroe office, just to the north. It wasn't the kind of town where kidnappings happen.

Conroe, with a 1990 population of 27,610, is the county seat of Montgomery County, and hub to many rapidly growing developments and towns. Lake Conroe is nearby, and The Woodlands, and a host of aggressively marketed upscale resort properties, most bringing in residents with income levels above the county median. But the city itself remains a small town, almost a scene from a Thornton Wilder play.

There's a courthouse in the town's center, ringed by small stores of questionable longevity, owing to the Super Wal-Mart out on loop

336. Most have already given over to law offices and small trendy restaurants that cater to the courthouse crowd. A half-block south, the Crighton Theater, complete with its old-style marquis, now houses the community theater. Around the corner is Tally's, the local domino hall, where, until it closed in 1999, old-timers gathered in the afternoons to talk of politics and the weather over the tinkle and clink of a half-dollar-per-hickey game of moon.

A block east of the courthouse lie the railroad tracks and, beyond that, older, more crime prone neighborhoods. There, a sense of despair hangs in the air like wood smoke. Other county residents drive through without seeing—without looking.

The neighborhood to which Wargo was called was on the opposite side of town, in the affluent Northwest area, where homes are spacious and comfortable, on wooded lots, with security lighting. Here, parents and children alike feel secure, safe inside homes well-protected with alarm systems and heavy deadbolts. Here, neighbors know and look out for each other. If a child had been abducted on this side of town, it was most likely for ransom.

In fact, Wargo had heard from the sheriff's office that there had already been a ransom call. He would need the details, the exact words of the caller, even vocal inflections. Sometimes officials with less experience might overlook minute details that could eventually help solve a case. With Wargo, checking all the details was routine.

He winced a little as he approached the house on Pine Springs Court. There was too much activity. Clearly, people were in the residence who shouldn't be. Well-meaning friends and family had gathered to show their support. Someone guided him through the visitors and introduced him to Carl and Paulette Everett.

"You're the parents of the missing child?"

Carl Everett appeared shaken but in control. He mechanically extended a hand. "Samuel McKay Everett is his name. He's twelve. We're his father and mother."

Wargo grasped Everett's hand in a professional manner. "I know this is difficult. I'll need to speak with you after I talk with the other agents."

Senior Agent Bill Jones had arrived a short time earlier, as well as FBI Supervisor Elizabeth Moore. The first priority was obvious—

controlling the crime scene. With the help of local officers, they asked those who didn't belong to leave. Some went across the street to the Kahn's residence, others next-door to Randy Bartlett's, where they might stay for an hour or two. But eventually, one by one, many wandered back. They wanted to see the Everetts, to share their burden and express their concern.

It frustrated Wargo. The crime scene was already contaminated. Footprints and fingerprints could have been obscured. Earlier, someone had made coffee for the guests, compromising the kitchen area. In addition, rather than keeping a low profile during the investigation, as Wargo would have preferred, the Everetts had made several calls, to whoever they thought could help or might need to know. Agents needed the parents of the missing child to be immediately available. It would help them focus on their investigation. It took almost twenty-four hours for Wargo to gain satisfactory control.

II

It was Wednesday afternoon before Crawford arrived back in Conroe. In his confused state, no sleep and laden with guilt, he thought he was covering his trail. He would go home and take care of other details: remove the Crown emblem, have the car detailed, take the bloody clothes to the cleaners, work out an alibi.

His movements were mechanical and thoughts came as impulses, no real thinking involved. He came home instinctively, to his life, his family, to the people and things he cared for. Without his family he would have no life. Leaving would never be a consideration.

Within minutes of arriving at home he received a phone call from the Schaeffers, his next-door neighbors. He joined them in their home and listened to the tragic story of McKay's kidnapping. Elizabeth Schaeffer was McKay's girlfriend and had been on the phone with him when it happened. She tearfully repeated the details. "He just said, 'Somebody's at the door,' and laid the phone down. He never came back." Crawford listened and nodded. He showed sympathy and concern. It was easy. He was close to tears himself.

Crawford stayed with the Schaeffers for only a few minutes. As he crossed the lawn back to his house, FBI agent Victoria Hale, in the company of another female agent, greeted him and identified themselves.

"You Hilton Crawford?"

He nodded.

"Have you heard about the abduction of McKay Everett?"

"Yes, I was just talking to the Shaeffers about it."

"We'd like to talk with you, if you don't mind." They were polite and friendly. It didn't seem like they suspected him.

Because of Roxie, the Crawford's Rottweiler, he went in through the back and opened the front door for the agents. "Can I get you anything, maybe a coke or something?" He tried to contain his emotions as they declined the offer.

Their first question was about a car that was seen leaving the scene. "Do you know anyone who drives a green or dark-colored Dodge?"

The question offered a tiny bit of hope. Maybe they wouldn't be able to identify his car after all. He assured them he did not know anyone with a vehicle of that description.

Then came questions about Amway. "How long have you been a member?"

"A few weeks, I guess."

"How many meetings have you attended?"

"I haven't ever attended a meeting. I don't really care much about that business. I just sort of let myself get pressured into joining."

"I know how you feel," one of the women said. "My husband thought about joining a couple of years ago. It just seems like the only people that really make any money are the ones at the top." She laughed.

"Why didn't you attend the meeting Tuesday night, though? You told them you'd be there. Where were you? Your wife said you went out of town."

He explained that he went out of town on business. He said that he had planned to leave after the meeting, but when Ronald McCurley, the employee who was to come with him, didn't show up he decided to skip the meeting and leave earlier. The last part was true. McCurley did indeed plan to attend the meeting with him, but had taken an afternoon nap and overslept, arriving late to Crawford's house. If he had been on time Crawford's intention was simply to accompany him to the meeting—a very big *if*. Crawford didn't think his accomplice, Remington, would even show up for the supposed "kidnapping." If he did, he'd just be stood up. There was no backup plan. Crawford didn't think he needed one. It hadn't seemed real. It was like a scheme made up by adolescent boys—one thinking the other won't follow through—daring each other and secretly hoping the plan won't be taken seriously.

The agents thanked him for his help and told him they might come back later that evening to talk to Connie.

Crawford was empty. He felt like the world was collapsing around him and he didn't know how to react. His first instinct was to go through the Chrysler again thoroughly. He spent more than an hour in his garage looking for anything that might have been incriminating. He removed the Crown sticker from his trunk and cleaned the vehicle. Over and over he cleaned. Exhausted, he went upstairs to his game room, to his Lazy Boy recliner. He wanted to sleep but he knew he couldn't. *Just try to think . . . focus . . . figure out what to do.*

III

Crawford became a police officer in 1961, long before the days of formal police training. He was told to buy a handgun, and decided a .38 special Smith and Wesson revolver seemed like a proper officer's gun. The department furnished his pistol belt and uniform. For training, he was given a card that explained the number codes the patrolmen used for radio communication. He was told to learn them, but not to worry if he forgot one or two, as they would "come naturally with use."

The duty officer led Crawford into Captain Kelly's office.

"Hello, Buddy." Kelly stood and offered his hand. A satisfied smile said that he too was glad that Crawford had chosen law enforcement. "It's good to have you with us. Did you learn your ten-codes?"

"Uh, yes sir, I think so," Crawford replied. "Uh, what does 10-21 mean again?"

Kelly laughed. "Don't worry about it—you'll learn. You're a natural-born policeman, I can tell by looking at you. I'm starting you off with Bobby Shaver and Norman Boone, two of our best. They'll show you everything you need to know. You need anything, you come to me. Good luck."

Crawford recognized the names. He had played varsity ball on the team with Bobby's younger brother, Larry. He was a year ahead of Crawford in high school, and had also been a Marine.

"Thank you, sir. I won't let you down."

A handshake—and Crawford was a policeman.

IV

Soon after the group was dispersed, Wargo questioned Carl Everett. Early in an investigation everyone has to be suspect, even the parents. He learned that Everett had been away all day, at work, and then at an Amway meeting. Afterward, several members of the group had met at the Village Inn for coffee. He discovered that Everett first became concerned when McKay didn't answer the phone for the second time that evening. He had tried to call McKay, first on his cell phone upon leaving the meeting, then again at the restaurant from a pay phone. Carl Everett had then excused himself early and gone home to check on his son. He left Paulette to ride with Randy Bartlett, a neighbor.

Wargo methodically considered the story while he took notes and compared it to versions given earlier in the evening. "What happened when you arrived home?"

"The uh, the lights were on and the door, the one around on the side there, was open. Not much, just barely, but it wasn't locked or anything." Wargo heard the noticeable quiver in Everett's voice.

"Go on," Wargo said. "Unless you need to get a drink of water or something—we can stop for a minute."

"No. It's okay. Like I say, I didn't know what was goin' on. I walked in and came right to the family room, and as I came in, the phone started ringing. I walked straight to it, never broke stride. There was a woman on it, a voice I didn't recognize."

"Can you describe her voice? Did she sound young or old? Any accent? Anything distinctive about it?"

"Yeah. Yeah. She sounded real throaty—raspy-like, kinda rough—ya know."

Wargo said nothing, offered no expression.

"Well, she asked me who I was and I told her. I said, 'This is Carl Everett.' Then she said, 'Where is your son?' " Everett hesitated, he sobbed.

"I said, 'He better be doin' his homework or eatin' dinner.' She said, 'Well, he ain't. We got him.' So I says, 'Who the hell is we?' and she says, 'It's just we, dammit, we got him, and if you wanna see him alive . . . .' I think that's about when I demanded to talk to him."

"What did you say?'

"I said, 'I want to talk to McKay!' I said, 'Let me talk to my son!' And she says, 'Well, you ain't goin' to. Just shut up and listen! If you wanna see your son alive again, you goin' to have to pay!' And so I told her to just tell me what they wanted."

Everett continued, telling Wargo the woman had demanded $500,000. She instructed him to bundle the money, using only hundreds, in stacks of $10,000. She said he would receive another call at 8 o'clock the next day with instructions on passing the money to them.

Wargo stopped him. "Did she mean morning or evening?"

"I don't know. She just said 8 o'clock. Guess I didn't think to ask."

The agent suspected she meant a.m. He would need to have the phones wired and ready by then. He made a quick call to get the technician on the way, someone to install the trap and trace. He would install the recorder himself. He nodded to Everett. "Please, continue."

"And then she said, 'And if you call the police, you won't never see your son alive!' But I told her, 'Well, if you won't let me talk to him, how do I know you've got him?' And she tells me, real nasty like, 'Well, you ain't gonna fuckin' talk to him!' Then she hangs up."

Everett told how after hanging up he frantically searched the house and grounds. He told of running to neighbors' homes to see if McKay was there. He told of standing in the street and screaming his son's name.

Paulette was too upset to be of any immediate help, so Wargo allowed her to be helped across the street to a neighbor's house until she could regain some control.

Next to be interviewed was Bill Kahn, from across the street. He had seen something—a car. It didn't seem unusual or out-of-place. He may not have even noticed had it not come close to backing into the garbage cans he had just put on the curb. The neighbor said he couldn't make out the car's occupants, but he did recall seeing an emblem in the shape of a crown.

"Dodge or Chrysler, Intrepid maybe," he told Wargo. "It happened right around 8:30 last night. It was pretty dark, but I think it was kind of brownish. Could have been a different color though. The windows were tinted. I couldn't see nothin' inside."

After daylight, agents took Kahn to a local dealership to see if he could pinpoint the make and body style. He walked the rows until he found a car like the one he'd seen—a Chrysler LHS.

Wargo had also noted that there were no signs of struggle or forced entry. Both he and Agent Jones thought from early in the investigation that whoever had taken McKay must have been someone he trusted, someone for whom he would have opened the door.

They asked the Everetts to help them compose three lists. The first would be a list of all the people McKay would have opened the door for. Number two was a list of all their friends who owned automobiles that might fit the description of the vehicle Kahn had seen. The third was comprised of names of all the people who were supposed to come to the Amway meeting. One name was glaringly present on each list—Hilton Crawford—so he became the obvious suspect.

V

Shaver and Boone, the Beaumont police training officers that Captain Kelly had assigned, made friends quickly with Crawford. They both knew his reputation as a high-school athlete, and were glad to be chosen as his training officers. Within twenty minutes they had shown him how to work the radio and what procedure to follow when doing so. It was around 10:30 at night when they left the station.

Shaver drove. He looked slyly at Boone. "Where should we go first, partner? What about Stedman's?"

Boone looked around at Crawford in the back seat. "Yeah. Stedman's it is. Buddy's okay. Let's show'm the ropes." Boone's face widened into a broad grin.

Crawford thought he must be the subject of a practical joke—an initiation of sorts. "You talkin' about Stedman's supply, out toward Silsbee? Hell, there's nothing out there but rabbits and possums, and a few stray dogs."

"Yeah. That's the point," said Shaver. "They like for us to stop by. Makes the employees feel safer to have uniformed policemen coming by late at night. And they don't have to pay a patrol service or hire a security guard." Crawford thought he saw Shaver wink.

Stedman's was a grocery supply warehouse a few miles out of town. By the 1990s the area would be swallowed by Beaumont's expanding suburbs. Fast food restaurants and convenience stores would line the area where only forest was visible in 1961, but Stedman's was still isolated when Crawford made his first visit.

Shaver turned into a concrete drive that led to the rear of the building, where three trucks were backed up to the dock. He parked just outside the loading area and the officers climbed a short steel stairway that led to a well-lighted warehouse floor filled with rows of stacked boxes. A half-dozen or so employees moved methodically from aisle to aisle with pull-carts and clipboards.

Crawford noticed two men standing behind a truck that was being loaded. One wore a driver's uniform, the other khakis and a white shirt. The man in khakis did all the talking while the other nodded and shifted his considerable weight from one foot to the other. The man in khakis saw the officers and nodded. He finished his conversation and came toward them.

He walked quickly, not like the others. His stride was long and purposeful.

"Buddy, this is Charlie. Charlie's the night manager," said Boone.

Charlie extended a hand. "Hey, I know you. You played ball for South Park. You scored seventeen points in that win over Silsbee. A policeman now, huh? I wondered whatever happened to you. Nice to meet you."

Crawford was accustomed to being recognized as a result of his high school athletic record. "Same here." Crawford shook hands with Charlie and felt his enthusiasm.

"Good to see you guys. Show Buddy around. I've got trucks to get out. Go ahead and get whatever y'all need."

Boone grinned at Crawford and nodded toward a pile of boxes. "Grab one of those and come with us."

The three uniformed officers strolled casually among pallets of canned vegetables and meats, racks of boxed candy, head-high stacks of paper goods and soft drinks.

"Like ham?" Without waiting for a response, Boone picked up three large canned hams and put them in Crawford's box.

"What goes good with ham? What about sweet potatoes? Yeah, yams and ham—that's the ticket. And green beans. Gotta have some green beans."

"Marshmallows?"

"Yeah, yeah, we'll put the marshmallows on top 'a the yams. Then we gonna need some mustard for the leftover ham—to make sandwiches." Boone was quickly filling the box. He helped himself to whatever foodstuffs he fancied.

Shaver laughed. "Leftovers? When the hell did you ever leave any ham uneaten?"

Crawford felt somewhat uneasy. He was apprehensive, but only for a moment. Boone and Shaver were good guys. Hadn't the chief called them two of his best officers? If it weren't okay, they wouldn't be doing it.

"And dessert," Boone said. "Gonna need desert. Hershey bars, that's the ticket. The kind with almonds." He took two out before adding them to Crawford's load. He put one in his shirt pocket and the other he began to eat. "Damn, I love these things!"

Crawford began to struggle. The box was becoming heavy enough to be difficult to carry.

"Shit, Norm. That's enough for tonight. We'll be back tomorrow," said Shaver.

They waved goodbye to Charlie, out on the loading dock. Crawford put the box of food in the police car's trunk and the trio resumed patrol.

Crawford leaned over the seat and keyed the microphone. "Unit 14 is 10-8," indicating that their unit was back in service.

VI

Crawford was still in the Lazy Boy when Connie came home from school. She came to check on him, to see if he wanted dinner. He said he wasn't feeling well, he wasn't going to eat. Minutes passed like hours and there was nothing, no thought that brought relief. The agents didn't return. He decided to tell Connie, to confess his crime to her and ask her forgiveness. He forced himself to rise and walk downstairs. He knew she would be in their bedroom, watching her soaps, the ones she taped during the day—it was her way of relaxing. He descended and moved toward the bedroom door, but the words wouldn't come. Instead of stopping, he went outside. For the better part of an hour he threw a basketball toward the goal attached to his garage. Whenever it failed to go in, he retrieved it angrily, as if the ball itself had behaved badly, had somehow failed in its responsibility.

Crawford came back inside, stopping at the door to the bedroom he and Connie shared. "I'm not feeling well. I know I'll be tossing and turning all night. I'm going upstairs to sleep in Kevin's room." Connie protested—they almost never slept apart while he was home. But he was adamant. "You need your sleep. I don't want to bother you."

In truth, he just couldn't face her. He closed his son's bedroom door and locked it behind him. And he cried. Connie knocked on the door to check on him at 10:30 and again at 1 a.m. He told her he still felt too bad, he didn't want to come down. He cried for hours, until the weight of his guilt smothered him, pushing him slowly into darkness.

The small amount of sleep that came made a huge difference. On rising, he felt more like himself. The guilt was still there but he was more in control. He would see this thing through. He would not deny his responsibilities. He rose, showered, and dressed for work as usual. He kissed Connie goodbye as she left for work. He loved her so much. He never wanted to hurt her or the boys. After she left he went into the back yard and sat on the edge of the deck. Roxie came to him. He hugged her and put his head next to hers and kept holding her until it was time to leave for work.

Crawford had been in his office around 45 minutes when FBI Agents Victoria Hale and Robert Lee arrived to question him further.

They began by asking more questions about Amway, but quickly moved to the question of his whereabouts Tuesday night.

Crawford tried to seem cooperative. He told them of going to Lufkin and then south through the deep piney woods of eastern Texas called the Big Thicket. It was the route he would have normally taken in order to check on his guards stationed in remote plants. Beaumont would have been his final destination. He gave the names of employees he saw at each of the plants. It seemed logical, but risky. The agents were pressing him, though, and he had to tell them something. After all, his people were loyal—they cared about him. He would call them and ask them to cover for him, to lie and say he'd been there. It was all he could think of to do.

Agent Lee was more aggressive in his questioning than the two women had been the previous day. He repeated questions and pressed hard for more details. He wanted exact times and places. He also quizzed Crawford about his personal life. "Do you go gambling at the boat in Lake Charles and were you there Tuesday night? Do you have a girl-friend in Beaumont that you might have spent a little time with?"

Crawford began to get frustrated. "I do go to the boat sometimes, but I wasn't there Tuesday night. I don't have a girlfriend. Like I told y'all, I got to Beaumont around two in the morning. I stayed at the Best Western on Eleventh Street."

The agents questioned him for almost an hour.

VII

While returning to the city, the Beaumont policemen took their first call of the evening, a family disturbance. It was the first of many such calls for Crawford during his career. Drunken, angry men—frightened, angry women—always anger, seldom regret. Regret would come later, after the officers had left. Sometimes there was violence. There was almost always the threat of violence. Crawford couldn't understand how people could be so cruel to each other, how they could let anger so completely dominate their emotions. The arguments would occur between husbands and wives, or between parents and children, family members who would the following day profess undying love for each other.

The two veteran officers taught Crawford to be wary of this type call. They cautioned him to never let his guard down. Many times patrolmen got careless around family squabbles since the subjects' rage was usually directed at each other rather than the investigating officer, a mistake that sometimes resulted in injury. With tempers already strained and judgment impaired, officers should always be on guard. In later years Crawford would himself fall victim on three occasions to attacks under similar circumstances. Twice he would incur stab wounds, and once he took a glass of household bleach in the face.

On this night, however, there was no blood. The call was nothing more than routine. All they needed to do was listen to the couple's grievances and offer common-sense advice. The couple only needed someone to referee and listen, a sounding board for temporarily skewed logic.

After working this call, they stopped at Rao's Bakery on Collier. The workers there were in the process of baking their nightly quota of cookies, cakes, and pastries of all sorts. Once again the officers accepted an armload of willingly given samples.

After Rao's they went to Ed Long's Barbecue. The manager there filled four sacks with a combination of ribs, beef, and sausage. There was a sack for each of them to take home and one sack for them to eat together.

Back on the road, Boone remembered bread. "Gotta have fresh bread with barbecue." Thus, their next stop was the Rainbow Bread Company, where the nightly baking was in progress. The aroma of freshly baked bread mesmerized Crawford. He thought it was the most wonderful smell he had ever experienced, even better than the pastries baking at Rao's. Each of the officers took two loaves and two packages of rolls. They were hot to the touch, and so soft they needed careful lifting.

During their feast of hot bread and barbecue, Crawford reflected on the night's events. Already he felt like he belonged. As a policeman, he was both respected and appreciated, which was obvious from the number of merchants who had offered them gifts. It wasn't graft. There had been no coercion by the officers. They had never asked for anything. Everything was given willingly, even enthusiastically. The storeowners and citizens knew the officers were risking their lives to keep them safe, and the gifts were simply a way to say thanks.

Their final stop was Daniel's Bakery on Port Street. This was the place for donuts. Every weekday morning they came sweet and hot from the cooking vats, so soft that chewing was almost redundant. Each man was given a dozen to take home and as many as he wanted to eat right away.

Back at the station, the officers divided the goods among themselves and transferred each share to their private vehicles. When Crawford arrived home, his father had already left for the morning shift at the plant and his mother was still asleep. He unloaded his trunk, but instead of putting items away in the pantry he left them on the kitchen table and went to bed. He was so tired he didn't even remove his clothes. Sleep came almost as soon as he felt the bed beneath him.

"Buddy . . . Buddy!"

His mother's voice was loud, it's tone sounded urgent. He was sleeping soundly, jarred awake so suddenly he knew something was very wrong. He sprang to his feet and ran in the direction of the voice, bumping the doorframe hard enough to shake the whole house.

"Buddy, what is this stuff? Where did it come from?"

Relieved that there was no real emergency, he smiled and rubbed his eyes. "It's just stuff, momma. It's stuff people gave us."

"They gave you canned hams? Vegetables? Why would anyone do that?"

"Those things came from out at Stedman's. They like it when we—when police officers come by and check on them. It makes'm feel better for their employees, being out there late at night and all. It's just their way of thanking us."

She was apprehensive. "It's not right. You can't be taking these things without paying for them."

"But, Momma, they want to give us these things. We don't ask for nothing. It's how they show us that we mean a lot to them, to the community. It wouldn't be right not to take it."

"Well—I guess, then. Sure looks like we won't be having to buy groceries for awhile."

Estelle Crawford was right. Their family did not have to buy groceries, at least not many. The merchant visits and the free goods were nightly rituals. All the officers participated. There was never any criticism. No one ever indicated that what they were doing might be wrong. And because no rules were broken, no crime or sin was committed, there was no guilt.

VIII

Within minutes after Agents Hale and Lee left Crawford's office, Agent Lloyd Dias called and told him they needed to check his car. "We need you to bring it here, to our office. Just need to take a few photos, comparison shots. It would really be a help to us."

Crawford protested. "I really can't now. I'm about to go to a meeting with a client. I could bring it in Monday."

Dias remained persuasive. "Monday won't do, Mr. Crawford. We need to see your car today. We're looking for a boy here, a child. Do you want to help in this investigation or not? I need to know!"

Crawford agreed to bring in the vehicle. He told Dias he would finish a few details and be in as soon as he could. He arrived around 1 p.m. While other agents went out to check the car, Dias stayed behind and interviewed Crawford.

"In regards to your vehicle, has anything been altered recently? Is there anything we need to know about?"

"Yeah. Well, maybe. I'm not sure whether you need to know this or not, but I had to take out the trunk liner."

Dias showed little reaction. "And why did you do that?"

"It was opened accidentally a while back, couple months or so. It was raining and the carpet got wet. It got mildewed and started to stink."

Dias, still expressionless, stared at Crawford.

He continued as if asked. "I talked to a woman called B.K. at the DeMontrond service center about replacing it. She'll remember talking to me."

"When was this?" Dias asked.

"A few days maybe. Or it mighta been a couple weeks."

Meanwhile, agents outside found the car had been recently washed. The trunk liner was missing, revealing clean, bare metal. More obvious evidence though, was the observation that a sticker had been recently removed. The Chrysler's paint was weathered to the point that it showed the pattern of a missing decal—a crown. It was the same decal Bill Kahn remembered seeing the night of the kidnapping.

These findings, the missing liner and the removal of the Crown emblem, led agents to conclude that it was indeed the car they were after. It was seized and taken to the county impound lot for further inspection. They gave Crawford a ride to the school so he could pick up his wife's car.

IX

Chief Willy Bowers, Beaumont's top cop when Crawford joined the police force, was more typical of the era than most would dare admit. Texas law enforcement entities were often left to decide for themselves which laws they really wanted to enforce. This led to so-called "wide open" vice operations in several counties, some of which were in Southeast Texas.

In Beaumont, Rita Ainsworth was a well-known Madame who ran most of the city's prostitution. She reputedly owned three hotels in the area and was a familiar name to all law enforcement in the region. On occasion, Crawford picked up bags of money and delivered them to Chief Bowers. The money supposedly came from a joint business venture between Ainsworth and Bowers—from a photo business operated by an employee of Ainsworth. Crawford never had actual proof, but he always believed the money represented payoffs. It wasn't his concern though. The Marines had taught him not to question his superiors.

Corruption among Texas law enforcement officers of the era was so rampant that it had led to the formation of the General Investigating Committee in 1959. Chaired by Menton J. Murray and Tom James, it was more commonly referred to as the "James Committee." The Jefferson County probe continued into 1961 and ultimately exposed corruption among local officials involving gambling and prostitution.

When the committee came to Beaumont, Hilton saw Willy Bowers give up friends and associates, but Bowers himself escaped indictment. Rita Ainsworth was forced to close her hotel operations, but she opened up again in her home, reducing the volume and profile of her business. But everyone, all the local lawmen, knew she was still in business, and they thought they knew who her benefactor was.

Crawford had never liked or trusted Bowers. So it surprised no one when, following a brief suspension in 1965, for what was termed "mistreatment of a prisoner," he left the force. He and his partner had made a drunk that was soaked in his own vomit ride in the trunk rather than inside the vehicle. He resigned and went to work for the Sheriff's Department. Not grammatical

Working for Sheriff R. E. Culbertson was an altogether different matter. He considered Culbertson to be a "good man," someone he truly respected. Nonetheless, by the time of his change, he had witnessed enough favoritism, even outright graft, on the part of law enforcement officials that he knew how the game was played.

Conseta "Connie" Parigi, the woman Crawford would come to love and share his life with, was attractive and popular. She was no cover girl, but she looked great in shorts. Buddy had thought about her often while he was away in the Marines. Officially, he was still boyfriend to another girl, Barbara May, but it was Connie who had occupied his fantasies. Thus, when he returned and found that Barbara had been dating other guys, he felt no disappointment, only relief.

His second day home he had decided to visit Connie's father's grocery on Avenue A. It was across the street from Stuart Stadium, where he and his friends used to stand and wait for baseballs. The Beaumont Exporters, a minor league team, played there, and during batting practice, if one went over the fence, the boys would chase them. They could then be exchanged for game tickets. He remembered that Connie spent most of her free time helping out in the family store.

"Hi. So you're home for good?"

She wore a white blouse with blue shorts. She was striking, perfect legs and a beautiful face. But, even more, her beauty was wholesome, virtuous and innocent.

(Forty years later, from his cell on Death Row, Crawford would still be able to describe exactly how she looked at that moment.)

"Yeah. I'm home. I thought about you. Would you . . . do you think you might want to go out with me?"

Unlike Barbara, Connie was shy. Comfortable only within her

own familiar world, she was dependent and pampered. Crawford offered her a life not unlike the one she had known, one that shifted life's burdens and skewed responsibility. He would be her protector, her provider, her paternal crutch, a role he accepted eagerly. Thus began their storybook romance. They hung out at the Pig Stand and drank cherry cokes and listened to Sinatra. From almost their first date, Connie and Buddy were exclusively a couple.

The romance was welcomed by both sets of parents. Connie's father had been diagnosed with cancer and made frequent trips to Houston for doctor visits. His future son-in-law would occasionally help out by driving him. It gave the two of them time alone, to get to know each other. It was during one such trip that the elder Parigi spoke his heart. "Buddy," he said. "I know you love my daughter very much."

"Yes, sir. I do."

"I want you to promise me something."

"Sure. Whatever you want."

"Connie is a very special girl. Promise me you will always take care of her—that you will make a good life for her."

"Sure. Okay. Of course I will."

"And there's something else."

Crawford waited.

"I'm very sick. I know I won't live much longer."

Another pause.

"I want to see the two of you married before I die. I want you to set an early date. Two or three months at the longest."

They had planned to marry, but not for a while. The old man's request startled Crawford, but it wasn't a bad idea. He already knew there would never be anyone else, and he wanted to please the people who cared for him—it was the natural thing to do. There would be details to be worked through. Wedding plans would need to be completed quickly. And there was the problem of Crawford's religious affiliation.

"Well, sir, we can try," he said. "I've sort of promised Connie that I'll convert, I'll become Catholic. I don't know if I can learn everything. I don't even know what I'll need to learn. Do I have to pass some kind of test or something?"

"Talk to Father Saco. He'll help get you through it."

X

Meanwhile, as Dias questioned Crawford, other agents had discovered his attempt to create an alibi. They learned that he had called security employees at several Louisiana Pacific facilities located throughout East Texas, attempting to convince or coerce them into saying he had been making rounds the night of the kidnapping.

An agent phoned employee Billy Tankersley and asked if Crawford had indeed been there on the night in question. "Yes sir. He was here all right. Delivered some uniforms." Should Tankersley's statement prove to be true, the theory developed thus far would be terribly flawed. Agent Ben Meyers was dispatched to question the witness in person. With the presentation of a badge the story changed. "No sir. He told me it would be a private detective posing as an FBI agent. I thought it was just a jealous wife, or somethin' like that. I never thought it was a real FBI person," he explained. "Why, if I'd known it was real, I never woulda lied."

In the case of another employee, Karen Dominy, agents attached a recorder to her phone and scripted a return call to Crawford. They prompted her to say that she had heard from the FBI and that they were coming for an interview. She was instructed to tell Crawford that she was scared, and ask him what to say.

"Well, just say I was there," Crawford told her. "I can't help if you didn't see me, I was there. I saw that other woman, the one that works with you. What's her name? Stacy . . . Stacy Robinson. She might remember seeing me."

Dominy told agents after the call that she did know the person he mentioned. "Yeah, I know Stacy. But Stacy Robinson's not a woman—he's a man."

Also on Thursday, agents with the Houston bureau division contacted officials with Houston Cellular for a list of calls from Crawford's cell phone. The record showed times and approximate location of the caller. He had made three calls to a Houston number, beginning at 9:10 on the night of the kidnapping. They showed that the first call had come from Conroe, the second from Beaumont and the last from Lake Charles, Louisiana, around midnight.

Phone records and employee statements confirmed what officials already knew to be fact—Crawford had lied. He had been nowhere close to the Louisiana Pacific plants he claimed to have visited. With evidence gathered thus far, agents had enough to go forward. It probably wasn't yet enough to convict, and McKay's whereabouts was still unknown. Thus, officials had to act quickly, opting for an early arrest. Tony Wargo, still monitoring activities at the Everett's, knew their best hope of finding young McKay was through Crawford. He would have to be convinced to lead them to the boy.

XI

Crawford called Father Saco in early July and explained his dilemma.

"Let me see, my boy. I want to make sure I understand correctly." The tone implied that he already understood. "You want to marry Miss Conseta Parigi. I can't fault your judgment—she's a beautiful young woman. From a fine Catholic family. But . . . let me see now . . . you say you want to become Catholic, but you don't have time for catechism. Hmmm. Yes, well, you say you can't come in on Saturday or Sunday because, let's see, you play semi-professional sports? Have I got it right thus far?"

Crawford didn't know if he should answer. He was beginning to regret he had asked. Nonetheless, he thought he heard a twinkle in the father's voice.

"I'll assume from your silence that I have understood correctly. Hmmm, yes, a definite problem, but not one that is unsolvable. Do you fish?"

"Sir? I'm sorry. What?"

"Fish—fish. The little scaly things that swim in the ocean. Are you a fisherman?"

"Well, uh, no. Not exactly."

"Ah, then, it will be your first lesson. No—oops—it will be your second. Your first is this: always turn to God, my son, and He will satisfy your needs. Be here at 6 o'clock, Friday morning."

Crawford took a change of clothes Thursday night, and as soon as his shift ended he met Father Saco. The boat was almost too big for the truck that was pulling it. The drinks were already iced and Saco smelled of suntan lotion.

"We'll be going for speckled trout today, my son." Saco busied himself with making sure the boat was secure for their trip to the Gulf. "But mind you we won't be throwing back the occasional redfish that might happen our way." He accented the second sentence with a wink.

The boat was impressive, at least twenty-feet long. It was white and immaculate, gleaming with the promise of adventure. Everything was in its proper place; the rods and ice chests were secured with straps. Crawford marveled at the similarities between boat and owner.

Father Saco's enthusiasm and wit caused time to quickly pass. The sun was well into the sky before he allowed the twin outboards to idle. The heat was oppressive, but flattened by a kind ocean breeze.

"This is the spot," he said. "This is where all the fish come to be caught."

Crawford followed Saco's example. He watched as confident hands selected a lure and tied it, then clipped away the excess line.

"That will be your side of the boat, my boy. Mind now, watch your casts. Make sure you know who's behind you. What we don't want to be catching here is one another."

Saco flipped the rod with little effort and the lure sailed outward, dropping with a tiny splash. Crawford watched as Saco worked the lure and tried to copy his movements. His efforts were clumsy by comparison, but Saco encouraged him.

"That's fine, son. You're doing well."

Before he had cast a dozen times, Saco struck his first trout. Then another, two throws later. His luck was considerable—and constant. All his movements were deliberate. Fish were removed from their barbs quickly, with accomplished dexterity, and his lure was confidently cast out again to work its charm in the blue-green water.

Crawford's luck was as bad as Saco's was good. It frustrated him to watch the priest continue to catch fish, while he caught none—not even a strike.

"What kind of bait is that you're using? Do you have another one like that?"

Saco smiled as he worked the lure. "I think perhaps there's

another, and you're welcome to it, but it won't matter. You'll catch fish only if God intends for you to catch fish. Remember when Jesus revealed himself to his disciples by the Sea of Tiberias? Simon Peter and his companions had been fishing all morning and had the same luck you're having."

He paused to set the drag and cast again.

"Well, Jesus called to them and said, 'Throw your net on the right side of the boat.' They did as Jesus said and caught more fish in one cast of the net than they could haul on board. They wound up having to drag them onto the beach."

He changed directions for another throw.

"You see, it's not what you use for bait that matters." He smiled. "It's what you have in your heart that makes a difference. If God wants you to catch fish, you will. Now take me for example. God knows that I have a sound Catholic heart and he wants me to catch these fish. In fact, you might even go as far as to say it's their purpose. God put these fish here so that I can catch them."

Saco turned and found Crawford listening intently, staring at him.

"What I can tell you is this, my son. When you become a good Catholic, you too will catch fish."

XII

Early Friday morning Crawford heard traffic moving outside. Not more than three or four vehicles, but even that was unusual for this residential street at 5 a.m. He glanced quietly out the window so as not to wake Connie, but everything looked normal.

Kevin had spent the night and had to leave early. Crawford heard him moving about the kitchen and came in to see him off. He hugged his son and walked him out. He had to leave soon as well. There were paychecks to deliver and he would have to make the entire route today. Minutes later, around six, he bent over Connie's sleeping form and kissed her softly.

He had backed only about halfway down his drive when the noise erupted. Police vehicles seemed to come from everywhere. The SWAT team was there, as well as at least five FBI agents. He saw at least eight pistols pointed toward him at close range. Others had shotguns and stood further back. The sirens, the yelling and confusion, had the desired effect. Crawford stopped immediately.

"Hands out the window."

"Exit the vehicle."

"Turn around and put your hands on the vehicle."

"Spread your legs."

He responded automatically. There was no thought of fleeing—there never had been. In his peripheral vision he saw Connie come running from the house. She wanted to know what was happening. She was still in her robe. One of the officers stopped her.

Roxie was very agitated during the commotion. She barked and snarled. Crawford heard someone say, "Shoot the dog." He tried to find where the voice came from as they leaned him against the car and cuffed his hands behind his back.

"Don't shoot her. She won't hurt nobody. Please, don't shoot her," he yelled. An officer told Connie to put the dog in the garage.

"Hilton Crawford, you are under arrest for the kidnapping of Samuel McKay Everett," someone said.

"I want to talk to a lawyer," he said in return to the faceless voice. The request was ignored.

FBI agents escorted the handcuffed Crawford through the back door of his home and seated him at his kitchen table. He sat sideways and rocked back and forth.

"I want to talk to Connie. Can I please talk to my wife for just a minute?" *Should have told her before. Should have told her that first night.*

The answer was a simple and firm no. One of the female agents took Connie upstairs.

Crawford continued the slight rocking motion. The movement was involuntary. *Everything is over. It's all fucked. Should have told her.* "I need to talk to a lawyer. Can I please call a lawyer?"

Agent Jones answered. "Not right now. We'll see about that in a little while. Right now we're interested in the whereabouts of McKay Everett. We need to talk about that first. Do you want to cooperate with us or not?"

"Yeah I want to cooperate, but I . . ."

"Are you going to talk to us?"

"Yes. I mean, I guess so. I . . ."

"Is there a better room for us? It's too crowded in here."

Crawford led them to the dining room table, where agents unlocked the cuffs and seated him. Agent Lee sat to his right and Detective Ervin sat to Lee's right. To Crawford's left was Victoria Hale, then Tony Wargo. Agent Jones completed the seating. They began by telling Crawford they knew about Billy Allen and that Irene Flores had been arrested.

Again he asked for an attorney. It was the third time.

Lee instructed Ervin to read Crawford his rights. He listened to the Miranda warning and signed the document, initialing each portion as instructed by Ervin. He signed the statement voluntarily, without reading or considering the consequences.

Agents began to question him even more vigorously. "We know you changed the tires on that Chrysler. Where did you buy the new ones?"

"I don't know what you're talking about. I bought those tires at Holmes Tire Company, about four or five months ago." Crawford was beginning to sweat profusely. Breath began coming in gasps rather than a steady rhythm. He felt himself slipping into darkness.

XIII

Crawford finally managed to boat two fish. With each catch Saco remarked, "The Lord's beginning to notice that you want to be a Catholic," or, "He's starting to see your potential." Still, Saco caught ten to his one. It was dark before they arrived back at the church.

While they fished, Saco had delivered what he called a "quickie" catechism. He gave Crawford a general overview. "God knows that you're busy protecting society and playing ball. That's His design, so He won't mind too much if you don't know everything."

One thing, however, that could not be overlooked or shortened was confession, and the obligatory prayers that preceded it: "Hail Mary," "Glory Be," and "Act of Contrition." Father Saco insisted that it be done immediately upon their return.

The two entered the darkened church as one might think of delinquent husbands who had overspent their privilege. They spoke in softened voices, through instinct, rather than design. Saco chuckled frequently, and his enthusiasm returned. Crawford felt a spark in the priest's personality similar to the one he had witnessed when they began to fish.

"There, my son. Through that door." He pointed. "That's where it will happen. That's the confessional."

Crawford nodded.

"Here. These are your prayers. Read them before you begin. Then, after you finish, say 'The Lord's Prayer.' You do know that one, don't you?"

Crawford entered the confessional from the dimly lighted church.

"Where's the light switch?" he asked.

"Light switch? Right, of course," Saco said. "You can't very well read without light, can you, my boy? But worry not. As I told you earlier, The Lord will answer your needs. However, sometimes patience is required. Wait there."

Crawford sat in blackness and listened to Saco's footsteps fade. A door closed. He sat thinking of how in the course of this day he had come to respect the priest. Here was a man who was devoted to God, of singular purpose, but willing to bend rules in order to accomplish that purpose. *Isn't this the way things should always be? Shouldn't the greater good be considered in any undertaking?*

An extended arm startled him from his thoughts. "And the Lord said, 'Let there be light.'" Saco thrust a flashlight toward him.

Crawford read the prayers, and Saco guided him through the confession.

"We're all sinners, my son. I am a sinner, but I'm here now as your priest. Search your heart for the sins you've committed. Confess your sins to me, and Christ will absolve you of your guilt."

For the next half-hour Crawford tried to recall his misdeeds: the candy bars he stole, the parent lies, the *if you let me use the car, I'll only go to the Dairy-Queen.* He was not better—nor worse—than any who have lived through two decades.

And then "The Lord's Prayer." It was recited in darkness.

Afterward they shook hands and Father Saco invited him to go fishing again the following week. Crawford thanked him and said he was too busy.

Saco smiled. "But, my son, the next time I guarantee you will catch fish."

Hilton and Connie married August 4, 1962. It was a huge affair, almost 600 people. Everyone who was anyone attended. Hilton's "I do" was followed by a knowing wink from Father Saco, a perfect climax for the perfect couple. Notions of anything other than *happily-ever-after* were inconceivable.

True to his prediction, Mr. Parigi died the following month. He passed comfortably, knowing his daughter would be forever cared for.

XIV

"Wake up, damn you." The room was dim. There were voices, excited, people moving. "You're faking, Goddamn you. I know God-damn well you're faking. Stop this horse shit and sit up and talk to us." The voice was that of Agent Lee.

It was coming back. The room was back in focus. He remembered. It was Friday morning, just three days since the kidnapping. Three days with hardly any sleep. Whenever he closed his eyes there was always something else, something he had forgotten, something he needed to take care of. He had cooperated, answered their questions, but they had caught him in lies. He had known they were getting close. They had impounded his car the day before. And now he was under arrest, was being questioned in his own dining room.

"Quit play acting. Sit up in that chair and talk to us. We want to know where McKay Everett is."

Crawford was silent now.

"We know you did it. We got your cell phone records. We know when you called Irene Flores and where you called her from. And she's cooperating with us. We got you. The only way you can help yourself now is by cooperating and telling us where McKay is."

"I want to cooperate. I just think I need to talk to a lawyer first." It was Crawford's fourth request for counsel since his arrest. "And I really need to talk to my wife."

"We'll let you call an attorney when we get down to the jail. So are you going to help us any more or not?"

Crawford remained silent.

"Guess that means you're not. Let's get him on down to the jail."

They rose, and Crawford was cuffed once again. "We're gonna' let you see your wife now for just a minute." Agents led him into the downstairs bedroom, where Connie had been brought minutes earlier.

Connie and Hilton, who had shared thirty-seven years of marriage, faced each other from a distance of four feet. There was panic and confusion in her eyes and manner. She was crying.

"That woman was so rude to me—she wouldn't let me call my sister to come stay with me. Hilton, what's happening?"

One of the agents answered for him. "He's being arrested for the kidnapping of McKay Everett. We think he may have killed the boy."

He wanted to tell her. He wanted to tell her he kidnapped McKay, but he didn't kill him. Agents were also in the room. He said nothing.

"We're going to take him on to jail. You'll be able to come see him later on today."

Crawford turned to Agent Lee. "I've still got those paychecks in my briefcase. These people don't make much money, and they need to get paid. Can I call my boss to come get'm."

The agents allowed him to call Marvin Keller and tell him the checks would be under his front door mat. He also had a further request. "Marvin, I've been arrested for kidnapping and they won't let me call a lawyer. Could you call one for me—just whoever you think is good?" The only attorney Crawford could think of to call was Jim Adams, the one who handled his recent bankruptcy. Adams was good with figures and books, but Crawford didn't know how much he knew about criminal law.

Keller was a true friend, very supportive. He had known Crawford for twenty years. He knew he had been under a lot of pressure over the past few years, but to think he could do something like this was inconceivable. He assured Crawford that he would take care of finding an attorney and delivering the paychecks. "Don't worry, my friend. We'll see you through this thing."

As he hung up the phone Crawford turned to Lee. "Could I ask one more thing from you?"

"What?"

"Could you please bring the car up close to my house?"

Lee ushered him toward the front door. "It's in front of the house. It's close enough."

In fact, the car in which Crawford would be transported was in front of a neighbor's house. He was walked, hands cuffed behind him, through his yard and the next. The sun, waking gently over the roofs, shined brightly against windows across the street. Morning dew was still on the grass and wet the shoes and pants legs of the agents.

Neighbors had heard. Curtains were pulled back, people came out into their yards and stared. The Browns were out and the Prices. The Schaeffers were out with their daughter, Elizabeth. She was crying. Some families held each other.

Everyone saw. They know. They must know. The looks on their faces—fear, disgust and something less than pity. It's like the dream. Now they know.

Part 3: The Interrogation

I

As husband and wife, Hilton and Connie Crawford settled into the fairytale life for which they seemed destined. He worked nights as a police officer while struggling through one more year of college at Lamar University. Connie continued to attend after Hilton dropped out. She got her degree and began teaching at a small Catholic school. And in 1964 their first son, Chris, was born.

Hilton—the name change, from *Buddy* back again to *Hilton*, came gradually—found life a seamless pleasure. As a patrolman on the midnight shift, the events of the first night never ended. Merchants were grateful and continued to offer their thanks with free merchandise and services. He met frequently with fellow night-shift officers for an early-morning round of golf. If they were on the course before 8 o'clock, they played for free. But even without the perks, money wouldn't have been a problem. He worked extra jobs, but it didn't seem like work. He loved the job, the feeling he got from being in a police uniform, like he was being paid for something he would have done for free.

Also, he tried out for, and won, a spot on Beaumont's semi-pro basketball team. The rivalry was never as intense as high school ball, but nonetheless, it was competition. And he was paid to play. He tried to remember to deposit the checks, but most of the time Connie would be the one to do it. He played two or three nights a week during the season.

Crawford loved being a father and husband. He wore well the weight of responsibility passed down by his own father. He aspired to emulate his father's strength and to suffer quietly the burdens of raising a family, no matter how great the challenge. He took Chris almost everywhere: grocery, barbershop, even the police station. They were together during the day while Connie was at work. On weekends they were a threesome—picnics, ballgames, social events—Crawford was proud of his young family. He wanted to show them to the world. To Crawford the term *father* was far greater than its biological meaning—it was almost spiritual, a sacred obligation.

II

Crawford was formally charged with the kidnapping of McKay Everett shortly after noon on Friday. Bill Jones, senior agent in the Conroe office, who coordinated the questioning, told Crawford they knew of his guilt and he could help himself by cooperating and leading them to McKay.

After officially charging Crawford, Jones contacted Agent Roger Humphrey from the Beaumont bureau office and asked him to interview Billy Allen, whom phone records indicated Crawford had talked with the morning after the kidnapping. In the company of another agent, Humphrey questioned Allen at his home in Buna, less than an hour's drive north of Beaumont. Allen was at first less than forthcoming regarding knowledge of Crawford's possible wrongdoings. After investigators left his home, however, he reconsidered and, within minutes of their departure, called asking them to return.

The second interview was more revealing. Allen told them that he had indeed seen Crawford on the morning in question. He related that the two had met in Lumberton, some twenty miles away at a storage rental facility he owned. He told of the removal of the Chrysler's bloodstained trunk liner and of a garbage bag containing items Crawford had asked him to keep. He remembered seeing a gun.

After the interview Allen led the agents to stall number 124. They recovered a green plastic garbage bag that contained, among other things, a Smith and Wesson .45-caliber pistol. On the hammer and the thumb guard was what appeared to be dried blood.

Crawford was questioned throughout the day Saturday. Although confronted with evidence that showed his apparent guilt, he remained silent. A television with fixed volume and channel was placed in his cell so that he could watch an impassioned plea from McKay's father. Authorities hoped it would help convince Crawford to disclose the boy's location.

III

The ball rose in an arch and, even with a visible wobble, flew in a spiral motion rather than tumbling end over end like the previous throw. It settled into Crawford's arms as easily as McKay's trust, the trust that comes from knowing someone for a lifetime. He complimented the grinning twelve-year-old on his improvement, a habit born of more than two dozen years of volunteer coaching. Give children guidance and praise them whenever they deserve it, reinforce positively. Crawford sincerely enjoyed helping young athletes, offering them advice. Their success was his as well. It was all that remained in the absence of his youth.

"Good throw. Keep the elbow in."

The advice was instinctual. Crawford's conscious thoughts were pervaded by the kidnapping. He knew what was going to happen, at least what was supposed to happen, but he didn't want to think about it. It was all planned, everything except the date. They would have to be flexible on that. But it needed to be soon; he couldn't hold things together much longer. All the bills, the money he owed, keeping things from his family, making sure no one knew his weaknesses—the stress was too much, too many people needed too much from him.

The stress caused Crawford's fainting spells to grow more frequent. They happened in his office and at home, even once on the freeway. He had recently spent several days in the hospital. In fact, that was why Irene Flores contacted him—she'd heard he was sick.

She liked Crawford very much. As her boss he had treated her well, had taken care of her and her family. There was trust and a caring friendship between the two. She called in early August and asked how he was doing. It was an ominous coincidence. Crawford had been wondering who he would get to make the ransom call. And his accomplice had suggested that the caller should be a woman.

IV

As Crawford was led, shackled, to the waiting police car, he walked with his head down, feeling rather than seeing the stares. The shame was unbearable. He had felt disappointment before, but never like this. The death of his parents, losing his business, a single night's loss at the tables amounting to more than a year's salary—in a strange way they had prepared him. They steeled him to the pain. From each recovery he grew more resilient, with each transgression more radical, more determined. Each desperate action fostered another. But he was not yet equipped for the hurt he now felt. He could not rid himself of his responsibility in McKay's death, yet he knew he must. Survival instinct outweighed remorse.

It was nearly 8 a.m. when he left his Rivershire neighborhood for the last time. Cuffed and in the back of a police cruiser, he squinted into the morning sun and tried to control his racing mind. He didn't know what he should do, but he could feel. *Never confess, regardless of guilt, always deny.* He knew the code, it was second nature to him. But he wanted to tell. He wanted to blurt it out. He wanted to shout that he was guilty and take them to McKay's body. It would be a way to end the pain. Nonetheless, he resolved to remain silent until he had spoken to an attorney and formulated a plan for his defense—he owed his family that much.

As Crawford was ushered into the Montgomery County jail facility, he once again asked for counsel. "I really want a lawyer. I don't know who, I just need to talk to one." The request was made to no one in particular, just to the suits and uniforms that surrounded him.

"Not right now," came the response. "We need to take care of a few things first."

Crawford went through the booking procedure and was locked in a cell by himself. Officers and agents made periodic visits, initiating conversations and trying to learn more about the crime and McKay's whereabouts. He tried to remain friendly but resisted the emotion that balled inside him. *By telling what happened it will end—it will ease the guilt—by simply telling.*

Almost two hours lapsed before he was allowed another attempt to retain counsel. He called Marvin Keller again and was told that Houston Attorney Don Flintoff had been contacted and was on his way. Somehow, it didn't help much to know he was coming. He wasn't already there, and Crawford needed desperately to confide in someone.

Perhaps agents sensed he was close to confessing. They continued to come to his cell and talk. It didn't seem like interrogation. They always began with unrelated things. The subject of McKay Everett would slide in later. No one except those responsible knew yet whether McKay was alive or dead. They needed Crawford to talk about the kidnapping.

One of the agents who visited him was Veronica Hale. "I just don't understand how you could get involved in this thing, Hilton. You're such a nice man. In a way, you remind me of my late husband." Crawford listened. Agent Hale had been very nice to him, and he liked her.

"My husband died three years ago. I miss him so much. I know the pain people feel whenever they lose a loved one. I know how much pain the Everetts must be feeling now. You're such a nice man . . . if there was a way . . . I know if there was a way you could help them without hurting your case. If there was something you could tell them, I know you would."

"I'm gonna give you something," he said. "If you wanna know what happened to McKay, you need to look for a man in New Orleans. His name is R. L. Remington." Agent Hale was on her feet and out of his cell in an instant.

V

Crawford had enjoyed his years on the Beaumont police force, but his job with the Sheriff's Department was even more rewarding. He was hired into the warrants division and quickly moved up the ranks to captain. In Texas, County Sheriff is an elected position, and as such, it was necessary for the department to maintain a positive image with the voting public. As an officer he continued to work cases, but he was also encouraged to involve himself in community affairs.

The latter responsibility came naturally to Crawford. He loved cultivating affection and gratitude, and he often worked with local charities and church groups. When the Sheriff's Department needed representation at any civic gathering, he was a ready volunteer. He also began coaching little league ball, a job he loved enough to continue for twenty-five years.

In 1968 his second son, Kevin, was born. By this time Connie was teaching in public school, and the roles for each of them, husband and wife, had become well defined. Connie worked in order to maintain her individuality, but after school it was very comforting to have an extremely attentive husband. Hilton did much, perhaps most, of the cooking, housework, and nuisance tasks. Connie responded to challenges in much the same way she did as a teenager, asserting herself with Hilton just as she had with her own father. Consequently, he was the one who performed the most annoying chores necessary to family life.

His competency as a Sheriff's Captain in charge of the warrants division was easily recognized. Under his direction, the department became known for its follow-up and the number of warrants cleared.

VI

In the weeks prior to the kidnapping and for the preceding year, Carl Everett talked frequently to Crawford about becoming an Amway dealer. Everett had joined through his neighbor and claimed to be doing very well.

"I don't know," Crawford would say. "I'm not very comfortable asking friends to join. It doesn't feel right."

"You're looking at this all wrong, Hilton. You're not really *selling* them anything. You're offering them a chance to make money, to make a *lot* of money. You're offering them the same chance I'm offering you, and in a few years, if they work at it and produce, they'll be coming back to thank you."

Everett wanted him to target his business associates, employees and clients. To Crawford it seemed like taking advantage. *I just don't want to do this. Some of them, the security guards, barely get by. I can't go out and ask them to obligate themselves for $30 or $40 every month.*

"I know you like to make money, Hilton, and I'm going to help you do just that. Didn't I help you before with the bank?"

When Crawford was trying to keep the security business afloat,

Carl had introduced him to his officer at First Bank of Conroe and helped arrange for a $10,000 line of credit, using Crawford's security company's receivables as collateral.

You did nothing special, Hilton thought. *You just introduced me.*

"Just look at us, at me and Paulette. We've worked hard building our down-line and it's paying off. Hell, Hilton," he said, whispering now, "I got two accounts. *Two accounts*," he repeated. "Over $500,000 in one and $750,000 in the other. Where can anybody make that kinda money nowadays? Who do you know that's got that kind of cash?" He hesitated. "Maybe Butch, but I'm guessing not even him."

The *Butch* Everett referred to was Butch Holmes, a successful big-time bookie and close friend of Crawford. Everett had gone on a couple of junkets to Vegas and Atlantic City with Crawford and Holmes, back in the 80s. Crawford recalled that Everett had enjoyed himself a lot, maybe a little too much. Maybe he felt guilty. Maybe that was the reason he didn't want to go again.

"Not even Butch, I'll bet. That's a lot of money. Wouldn't you like to have that kind of money, Hilton? Don't say no. Don't say you don't want it, cause I know better. I know you better than that."

Crawford never really said no. The word never came easily for him. He just kept saying he would think about it. Connie was the one who finally erased any resistance. "Hilton, why don't you just go ahead and write him a check. It's not a lot of money, a couple of hundred dollars, and they're our friends. Just write him a check and he'll quit bothering you. And you can quit obsessing."

Connie didn't know how bad off they were financially, and it would have been embarrassing to admit that he couldn't afford the $200. So Crawford became an Amway dealer, at least in the technical sense. He never actually sold anything or attended any of the meetings.

Writing the check wasn't the end, it was more like the beginning. Now Crawford was expected to sign up other people, to talk to everyone he knew, to tell them what a good opportunity Amway was. He was encouraged to go to the meetings so he could see for himself, and he could tell the others. Going to meetings would help him understand how it worked and would infuse him with the Amway enthusiasm, so he could focus on the American dream. Carl Everett had the focus, and the enthusiasm—he wanted to share it with Crawford.

"I'm gonna help you with your down-line, Hilton. I'm gonna sign up some people for you, help you get started. Once you see how much money can be made and how easy it is, you'll really get into it. People like you, Hilton. You're a natural, and you'll be doin' them a favor. Like your employees, I know you wanna see them make more money."

"Yeah, but a lot of'm, they really can't afford it. I don't want to talk'm into buying something they—"

"Hilton, you're looking at this all wrong. Let me ride with you when you make your rounds, talk to your employees. Remember, you're doing them a favor."

Crawford didn't like the idea. He thought he had said no, but Everett showed up anyway, at 7 a.m., just as Crawford was getting ready to make his rounds. He had boxes of pamphlets and promotional material. Crawford tried to be polite. He took the materials, letting Everett put them in his truck, but he stood firm on riding together. He would not let Everett canvas his employees.

VII

One deputy in whom Crawford had special confidence was a young African-American named John Bassett. Officer Bassett was commonly Crawford's choice for partner—he needed someone he could depend on in tight situations. The two became close enough to frequently share dinner in each other's homes.

One case the two of them worked together was a "worthless check" warrant, served in one of Beaumont's depressed neighborhoods. The house was a shotgun-style row house badly in need of paint. A large woman with an Afro-style hairdo answered the door and let them in. At first, she denied being the person they were looking for.

"No, suh!—that's not me! It's my sister you want."

Crawford wasn't convinced. He gave Bassett a nod to proceed with the arrest, but she was too big and strong. She slugged Barrett and shoved Crawford out of her way. Crawford lunged as she ran through the doorway to the second room. He grabbed hold of what seemed easiest to grip—her hair—and braced himself, expecting a struggle that never came. Instead, he was left holding a wig.

Barrett recovered quickly and was close when Crawford caught up with her in the last of three rooms, the kitchen. This time he held her by the left arm, while her right flailed wildly. As Barrett moved into position to help subdue her, her right hand closed on an open container of Clorox. She slung it, striking both officers squarely in the face.

Later, after the toxic fluid had been purged from eyes and skin, Crawford sat in the emergency room watching the color fade from his expensive new sport coat. "John," he called to the adjoining cubicle. "Looks like this turned out to be your lucky day."

"How so?"

"Well, I know how much you've always wanted to be white . . . ."

It was the kind of joke that could be shared only by friends who were close enough to trust each other with their very lives.

VIII

"Keep the elbows in and concentrate. Take your time and focus on the receiver. You're doing good, really good." The kidnapping would be soon. It had been agreed. Crawford tried to force the thoughts from his mind and concentrate on the advice he was giving.

McKay looked at him. "Thanks for playing with me. I really think I'm getting better."

Inside the Crawford home it was comfortable and cool, nothing felt of the 100-degree August afternoon. Crawford toweled sweat from his face and arms. "How 'bout a Grapette?'

"Yeah—great!" McKay's enthusiasm was one of his most obvious characteristics. A glimpse into the glimmer of his child-eyes said quietly: This one is well loved.

The drink they shared was a grape-flavored soda in a small hourglass-shaped bottle. It had been a popular soda when Crawford was McKay's age, but had become a modern-day rarity. Crawford, though, had found an independent grocer in rural East Texas that still stocked it. Whenever he made his rounds checking security at the lumber plants, he would buy some—as many as five cases at once.

"Pretty good, huh?"

"Yeah! Super!" Life was still an adventure for McKay.

Crawford turned the hand holding the football to see the barely-visible inscription, "From Uncle Hilty." It was written with marking ink, now so faded he could hardly see the words. He had given McKay the football months earlier, but he couldn't remember the occasion. Maybe it was Christmas? Maybe . . . ?

The other adults had stayed inside. McKay hoisted himself onto his father's lap. "Uncle Hilty's been showing me how to throw a spiral. He says I'm doing really good." Carl responded by giving his son a bear hug.

Connie spoke. "Hilton, Carl just reminded me that we need to go to one of his Amway meetings."

"That's right, Hilton. Just signin' up and buying the product isn't making you any money. We need to work on your down-line. You need to attend some of the meetings, and bring some prospects. I'll help you with'm."

"Yeah. I been thinkin' about it."

"Don't just *think* about it. You gotta *do* something about it. With all the people you know, networking'll be a snap. You can build an organization in no time. You got a good opportunity to make some money. You just have to make up your mind to do it—just do it."

Crawford pitched the football to McKay. "Yeah, okay. I'll call around and see who I can round up. I'll get somebody to come." Unsmiling, he looked away, avoiding Carl's gaze.

"Good. You won't regret it. This is your first step toward financial independence. I know your decision is going to have a great effect on both our futures."

Crawford only looked at him and nodded.

Carl pushed himself out of the chair. "It's time to go, son. Give Hilton a big hug."

McKay embraced Crawford.

"Good to see you too, McKay. Keep working on the arm." Crawford turned toward the kitchen and sighed.

"Hilton," Connie called from the doorway. "Aren't you coming to see them off?"

IX

Crawford's question for Flores, the woman he wanted to make the ransom call, was simple and direct: "You want to make some quick money? $25,000. All you have to do is make a phone call."

In spite of the fact that Crawford had never before asked her to do anything illegal, it was obvious that this would be something against the law. She didn't know what. It was just a phone call, so it couldn't be too bad. Hilton wouldn't be involved in anything too serious. It'd be safe—Hilton always had everything covered. No shockers like the drug sting.

Flores had been a good employee for Crawford before she caught her case, and the two had stayed in touch. Her security career had ended when she was sentenced to fifteen years for delivery of cocaine. A friend's husband had set her up in order to beat a case of his own. It was the biggest deal she'd done, a kilo. She didn't know the people, but her friend's spouse swore he'd known them for years, that they even went to high school together.

When they appeared, it seemed like they came from everywhere at once, men with DEA on their jackets. Guns. All pointed at her. She served eighteen months in the Texas Department of Criminal Justice before she was paroled. Unfortunately, though, there's no parole from life on the outside as a convicted felon. She had family and responsibilities. *$25,000 for a phone call?* She wondered if it wasn't a trick question.

Flores said she was in. Crawford gave her no more information at the time. They met in early September and discussed the details. He gave her only the names Carl and McKay, along with a phone number. He told her exactly what she was to say: "We have your son. If you want to see him alive again, it'll take a half-million dollars. We'll call you with delivery instructions tomorrow at 8 o'clock." Simple enough. He told Flores that the boy's mother was in on it, that she wanted to leave her husband and this was the least complicated way to extract money from the relationship. He said the mother would be picking up the boy in Louisiana.

"It's just a domestic con game. She wants to leave with her kid and needs the money to get away." Flores believed him. It sounded like just the kind of scheme Hilton would be involved in.

"He was always like that—helping people," she later recalled. Even after receiving a twenty-five year sentence for her role in the crime, she still claims to feel no resentment toward Crawford.

Two more hours passed after Crawford was led to his cell in the Montgomery County Jail, and still no attorney came. Finally, he was allowed to call Marvin Keller again.

"Hilton, he should have been there by now. I don't know what happened. I'll try and reach him again and see why he's not there," Keller said. The attorney Keller had contacted, Flintoff, was in fact, not on his way. Crawford later heard that he came the following day. He never knew for sure whether or not the attorney came at all.

Crawford became more desperate. As the afternoon minutes slowly passed, he became obsessed with finding an attorney to talk to, any attorney. He wanted to do something—to tell—or not tell—he wanted to decide. He needed a lawyer. The only attorney Crawford knew to call was Jim Adams, a seventy-seven-year-old tax specialist that Crawford had used to file bankruptcy.

Adams came that night. Crawford was uneasy about the attorney's competence, but he was in a difficult situation. He had virtually no money and very few assets. He needed counsel, and Adams was willing to take his case. "Can you handle it, Jim?" Adams assured him he could. "You know I don't have any money, don't you?"

"Don't worry about the money, Hilton. We'll work all that out."

Hilton gave Adams the details of the kidnapping. However, he left out the fact that McKay was already dead. "Remington was supposed to put him on a bus whether or not we got the money, but I don't think that's what happened."

"You don't have to worry about what you *think* happened. If anybody asks you, just tell'm he's supposed to be on a bus."

"I don't think I should do that. I don't want to get people's hopes up." Crawford didn't want to lie and claim that McKay was still alive. *Sometimes it's confusing—the right and the wrong of things—and when and how to stop the lies.* He finally agreed to say nothing for the time being.

Adams instructed the officers that Crawford was not going to talk anymore that night, and he was led back to his cell. They kept him on what deputies told him was a "suicide watch," and checked him every few minutes during the night, waking him each time. Deputies shined their flashlights into his face and called his name. They had to see him open his eyes. Sheriff Guy Williams also stopped by a couple of times, in case there was anything he wanted to say.

XI

After achieving the rank of captain with the Jefferson County Sheriff's Department, Crawford's responsibilities included acting as liaison with community leaders; he made friends easily. One such friend was John Powell, an executive with Conn's Appliances. Both men were avid golfers, and both shared a sense of civic duty. They often teamed together in charity tournaments.

Also shared was their love of life and laughter. Both men displayed an ease that came from being comfortable with one's self. They once picked out a washer and dryer to be given to a needy family by a local charity. Together they walked Conn's appliance showroom looking for the set that would best fill the family's needs. Powell stopped in front of a likely looking washer. "How bout this one? Think it'll do?"

"Well, it's big enough," said Crawford. "But I don't think we should spend that much money."

Powell kicked the edge of the bottom panel and turned to Crawford. "It's got a little dent. We'll have to discount it."

"My, so it has. I didn't notice that before. Yeah. I think it'll fit our budget after all."

(The bond between Powell and Crawford lasted more than two decades—until the kidnapping.)

Crawford made other friends, men like W.L. Pate, who owned the Chrysler dealership, and Tommy Rochelle, who owned Rock's lounge and the Best Western motel, the same motel he checked into the morning after the kidnapping. Crawford was welcomed into this circle of men who, unlike men of his father's ilk, seemed able to mold life to fit their needs. The common link was that they were all successful and happy, living lives that seemed like a long, comfortable adventure—an unending trip to Disneyland. Crawford felt good being one of them.

Another thing the men had in common was that they enjoyed gambling: wagering on their frequent golf games, betting on sports—

football, basketball and baseball, in that order. And they enjoyed an occasional trip to Vegas: golf in the daytime, craps and blackjack at night. Life at its fullest.

In fact, Rochelle even ran junkets. He put together groups of local businessmen for trips to the Riviera Casino. It was in the days when casino bosses catered to groups like his. Everything was complimentary—airfare, hotel, everything. Crawford was, of course, included.

He couldn't go often. He didn't have the time. Besides, his financial circumstance was different than the others—he didn't own a business in which he could manipulate cash flow. Still, he was good at picking sports winners. After all, he knew a lot about the sports themselves, probably more than any of the others. He bet locally and usually picked up a little extra to use in the casinos.

They called Crawford the Sheriff. It was sort of a nickname only used by the group. When he was introduced to their contacts in Vegas, it was always "Meet the Sheriff," or "Say hello to the Sheriff." One of the men they introduced him to was Vic Vickery, a manager at the Riviera. Vickery was the one Rochelle ran junkets for.

Having a law enforcement officer as a junket guest did not go unnoticed by casino executives. In late 1968 one of them called him. A customer with a local address had written a bad check for $10,000. Would he mind helping them out, giving the guy a call? They just wanted their money. It didn't seem to Crawford to be an unreasonable request. He was in the warrant division. It was his department that would serve the guy anyway. He could even save the county some legal fees. He made the call. Soon other casinos followed. He was contacted every couple of months, anytime some deadbeat from Jefferson county wrote a hot check to beat a heavy tab.

Crawford never accepted money for helping the casinos. He was doing his job; he was just doing it maybe a little more efficiently for them. In turn, the casinos showed their appreciation. His status was elevated to VIP. He and his group of friends were shown greater hospitality, more "freebies," more attention. Likewise, his acceptance within the group of men he so admired was guaranteed.

XII

On Saturday morning, after being awakened at regular intervals all during the night for "suicide watch," a deputy moved Crawford to a bullpen-type cell. "Bring your mattress, there ain't no bunk in here," the deputy told him. It was a large cell, empty except for a television that had been moved in. He didn't understand. There was no volume or channel control inside the cell. An announcement blared through the jail speakers. "News Bulletin," the voice said. "Local man held in the kidnapping of young McKay Everett. The child's whereabouts is still unknown."

The first image Crawford saw on the screen was Connie. She was crying. She pleaded with the camera. "Hilton, please, if you know anything you can tell them about where McKay is, you've got to do it. Please help the Everetts find their son."

The scene cut abruptly to the Everetts. The voices were loud. "I want to talk to Hilton," Carl Everett said. He stood before the microphones holding a football that had been a present from Crawford. An inscription written in marking ink was shown to the camera. It read "From Uncle Hilty." Crawford saw the words. He remembered playing ball with McKay just weeks earlier and they were hardly visible. Later he learned that Carl had retraced them for the television audience.

"Hilty, something's happened. I don't know what, but there's been a lot of people involved. But there's one still missing and that's McKay." Everett's voice shook as he fought away the tears. "I just want you to search down deep in your heart. Whatever did happen, I hope your heart will soften and understand that all we really want is for McKay to be back home and safe. In my heart I know that you would never harm my son. You loved him like your son. You gave him this ball. He called you Uncle Hilty, and he loved you dearly." Everett went on. He mentioned the family visit three weeks earlier when Crawford had played catch with McKay. He said that McKay "hugged you and kissed you on the forehead," as they were about to leave. The taped broadcast was played over and over with the volume at extreme levels. The words rose and penetrated his flesh like the voice of eternal damnation—and Crawford felt small and worthless.

During the afternoon Sheriff Williams came to Crawford's cell. "Hilton, your boys are here. They want to talk to you."

He was led to a visiting area, a glass-enclosed room with cold metal tables, where Kevin and Chris were waiting.

"Dad, we love you. We're gonna help you get through this," Kevin said. Crawford had trouble choking back tears. He nodded. "They've asked us to talk to you. They've asked us to see if you won't help them find McKay."

"I just don't know. They were supposed to put him on a bus. He might be on a bus on the way home." He would carry the shame of lying to his sons on this day for the rest of his life.

Even the hardest of criminals might have broken, especially feeling the effects of sleep deprivation. Crawford's thoughts were unclear; he no longer had any concept of what day it was. The desire to confess was overwhelming. In the evening hours, sometime after dark, maybe around 9 p.m., Sheriff Williams returned. "Hilton, I'm just on my way home. Do you need anything?"

Crawford respected Williams, his dedication. He appreciated the kind voice.

"I just want you to know that, if you want to talk about anything, if you want to get something off your chest, just let one of the deputies know. They can get me anytime, day or night, and I can be here in just a few minutes."

Crawford nodded and hung his head.

It may have been the personable manner of Williams—or maybe he had simply reached his limit. Within minutes after the sheriff left, Crawford decided to take him up on the offer. He asked one of the deputies to put a call through to Williams. He said he wanted to talk. "I want to talk to my wife first, though," Crawford told Williams. "Can I call my wife and my lawyer?"

After talking to Crawford on the phone, Adams spoke briefly with Williams and told him that he thought his client was ready to make a statement. He said he would be there as quickly as he could. While Crawford waited, he prayed and felt relief. *It's going to soon be over.*

Connie went in first. He was so ashamed. *Holding her feels wrong—like she might somehow become contaminated.* "I want to tell you what happened."

Silence followed. Still, he could not force the words.

She looked at him. "Hilton, is McKay all right?"

He shook his head and averted her gaze. "McKay's dead." It was finally said. The rest would be easier now.

"Oh, no," she said softly. "Oh God, no."

"Your lawyer's here," someone called from outside the cell door.

Adams found husband and wife sitting together, both in tears. Crawford told of the murder and of the events leading up to it. Adams listened intently, while Connie sobbed and rocked gently, her arms folded tightly across her chest.

After all was said, Adams inhaled deeply. "Well, you can't say anything about this to the authorities—not at this time."

Connie interrupted. "He's goin' to tell! He can't let those people go on thinking their son is alive."

"Hilton, listen to me. I'm advising you not to say anything. It's not in your best interest."

"I feel like I have to."

"He's going to tell," Connie repeated. "He's got to."

Adams shook his head.

"I just think . . . nobody's going to have any peace unless I tell. I'm going to tell them. I have to put this thing to rest."

Adams resisted. "I told you it isn't in your best interest. If you're not going to listen to my advice, there's no use in me being your lawyer."

"Maybe you're right, but it's my decision, and this is what I'm gonna do. If you feel like you have to resign, that's up to you."

"Well, if you're determined to do this, at least let me talk to someone first and see if we can't make sure this will be tried in the federal system. You'll stand better chance there than in state court."

Crawford agreed.

Adams returned within minutes. "Okay, it's all set. Do this, if you feel like you have to."

In fact, it was not "set." Adams had spoken only with the FBI agents who, they later found, had no authority to promise a federal trial. District Attorney Dan Rice made that very clear after Crawford confessed. By then, however, there was nothing further Adams could do. But it mattered little. By the time he confessed, Crawford could wait no longer. He had to tell. He had to dull the sadness.

Part 4: The Confession

I

When Connie left her husband's cell, officers noticed that she was visibly shaken. She was crying and obviously had been for a while. In her right hand she held a wad of tissues that she moved from one eye to the other. Her left hand crossed her body and grasped her other arm just above the elbow. Both arms were clinched tightly to her torso, as if the pressure might somehow stay her sorrow.

After Connie left the interview cell, Adams entered. Client and attorney spoke for several minutes before emerging. When their conversation was done, Crawford and Adams, along with Sheriff Williams and Agent Jones, moved to a different, larger interview room.

The officers were silent as Crawford disclosed that McKay had been killed. He went on to describe what he claimed were the true circumstances of the kidnapping. He said an accomplice named R.L. Remington had murdered McKay, and he drew a map for the officers pinpointing the location of McKay's body. It would lead officials to a remote exit off I-10, deep in Louisiana's Atchafalaya basin, called Whiskey Bay.

II

In Jefferson County, both professional and civic groups responded eagerly to Captain Crawford's community involvement. In the early seventies, the Black Peace Officers Association of Jefferson County made him their choice for Officer of the Year. During the following year, the 100 Club honored him as their choice for top-cop as well. Crawford's warrants division became a showplace of the department. They consistently cleared impressive numbers of cold-case files, as well as current warrants.

County politicians also noticed Crawford's performance. His father was a long-time precinct chairman for the Democratic Party, and as early as 1972 both father and son began receiving feelers from local political leaders. They insisted that Crawford was a cinch to win the race for county sheriff—a hometown boy, exceptional high school athlete, ex-marine with an outstanding law enforcement record—what better qualifications could one have?

Their arguments were convincing. If Hilton had created a dream-life for himself, he probably could not have created a more idyllic scenario than the one he already lived. But the clamor of the crowd was still in his head. The noise and excitement—all focused toward him—he wanted it again. It's addictive—the rush, the competition, risking everything and coming out on top. In August of 1975 he left his perfect life for another chance to become the public's hero, the way he had been in high school. He resigned in order to run against Sheriff Culbertson.

Crawford campaigned for the better part of a year. Despite his excellent record, he was running against a popular incumbent. He had been convinced that he could win easily. He had listened to the people who encouraged him, who told him what he wanted to hear. Their optimism was enough for

~70~

him—their motives were not questioned.

But in politics, as in love, bedmates can be fickle. Promises went unfulfilled. Supporters who were at first steadfast wavered with time. Contributions slowed, and all but disappeared.

Crawford was undeterred. But without an income, and with continuing campaign expenses, money became a problem he had not foreseen. He borrowed heavily against all his assets. When he reached his limit with creditors, he turned to family and friends. Even so, he could not bring himself to tell them how badly he needed the money; appealing to sympathy was never an option.

In spite of Crawford's money problems and political inexperience, the race was close. When the tally was in, he had lost the election by only 1043 votes out of more than 90,000 votes cast.

(Culbertson did not forget the election, or his opponent. More than twenty years later, after charges of kidnapping and murder had been filed against Crawford, he publicly voiced his surprise. He remembered Crawford as being a very capable law enforcement officer.)

III

During the 1980s Crawford went to Vegas three or four times a year. Dean Harrell, a manager at the Dunes Casino, had become one of Crawford's closest friends. Crawford and any of his guests could almost always get comped by Harold, not because of high-roller status, but because they were buddies.

Crawford also became close with a friend he met in Conroe, Butch Holmes. Holmes was a bookie, a big one, maybe one of the biggest in Texas. But he wasn't a mafia-type character. On the contrary, he was a businessman, one who liked sports and liked to gamble, and who combined the two into a successful, albeit illegal, business.

Men like Holmes, bookies who cultivate a large clientele booking sports bets, are not usually like movie stereotypes. Not greasy, underworld types who send out their tough guys to break legs. Usually they're honorable—the successful ones. They pay off when they lose, and when they get stiffed, they write it off like any other expense. The industry doesn't lend itself to a lot of negative publicity. Players who get strong-armed often complain to the police, and that creates too many problems. Holmes was a model for success in his field. He owned his own plane, and even had a federal gambling stamp.

Both Crawford and Holmes enjoyed sports, as well as gambling on the events. They went to Vegas together, played blackjack, shot craps, bet sports. It was great to be in Vegas for the big sporting events, like championship fights or bowl games on big-screen. Crawford even introduced him to his good friend Dean Harrell at the Dunes.

Holmes had a connection in New York who relayed insider information on sports teams. He used the data to bet heavily on games, usually football or basketball. Crawford was so well trusted that Holmes confided in him, sharing whatever he knew. In return, Crawford made bets for Holmes in his own name (lay-off money) so that other bookies wouldn't know the bets came from Holmes. The arrangement became a second income for Crawford. During football season he might make as much as two thousand a week. Basketball was lucrative too, but it made him only around half as much. The arrangement continued for much of the 1980s.

In 1986 Crawford met Billy Allen, another man who would later influence his destiny. The two were introduced by their mutual friend Gary Capo and quickly became close. Allen was close to Crawford's age. Graying and rotund, with a sparkle in his eyes to match his sense of humor, he was the kind of man for whom Crawford had instant admiration. He was self-confident and self-sufficient, living by his own code in a world of rules. He wasn't a drinker or womanizer, both character traits that Crawford disliked. Yet he was one who believed that life should include daily pleasures.

For Allen, life was a game. He lived by his wits, unafraid to offer unconventional solutions to conventional problems. His lifestyle was opportunistic, almost picaresque.

Allen's business of record was storage rental. He owned several centers in the small towns north of Beaumont, including the one in Lumberton, where police later found the murder weapon. And he was a racehorse owner who frequented Louisiana tracks like Evangeline Downs in Lafayette and Louisiana Downs in Shreveport. Crawford later learned that Allen and his brother had both been barred from Louisiana racing because of their misdeeds.

One reputed scheme involved manipulating the racing times of one of their thoroughbreds, a horse called Off to the Races. In collusion with jockeys, they were said to have intentionally held the horse to a string of losses while waiting on the odds to increase enough to make a big score. When they decided the time was right, they stationed cohorts with cash for wagering at off-track betting centers around the country, chiefly Las Vegas and Atlantic City. They couldn't have bet enough at their home track to make it worthwhile—it would have diluted the odds, lowering them enough that the scheme wouldn't have paid off. Crawford heard that they wagered almost $100,000, at odds of around ten to one. They would have pocketed the better part of a million. And who was hurt? OTB's? Casinos? Sports-betting parlors? No one who would incur sympathy.

Off to the Races was fast, too fast to be a claimer. It's likely the Allen brothers didn't find out until it was too late, though, to plan a racing career for him worthy of his speed. The purses he would have been eligible for wouldn't have been nearly as profitable as exploiting his record for the sake of one huge payoff.

Afterward, as a result of an investigation by the Louisiana racing commission, the horse was sold at auction. Reputedly, ownership of Off to the Races worked its way through a number of different buyers, ultimately returning to the Allen brothers. They knew the horse's capabilities. And the scheme worked too well the first time not to give it another try. They kept their ownership of the horse a secret until they figured a way to get it back into action.

Crawford was a key player in the horse's comeback. They transferred ownership to him so it could run in Texas. Off to the Races ran in Sam Houston Race Park's inaugural season. Once again the horse won and paid great odds. Crawford's first experience as a racehorse owner was a profitable one.

Pat Foster, the University of Houston basketball coach, was another friend of Crawford's. The two had been close since the old days in Beaumont, when Foster coached at Lamar University. An obsessive love of sports was their common interest. Crawford was an active supporter of the Houston Cougars when Foster was coach. He helped with recruitment and player morale. During holidays, if players weren't able to go to their own home for one reason or another, Crawford sometimes brought them home with him. For those short periods, the Crawfords became the players' surrogate family.

Crawford traveled with the team, expenses paid. Games in California, Ohio, Illinois—if it was convenient and there was room on the plane, he went along. He wore a hat and sweats with the team logo, just as if he were an official with the team.

Foster was also helpful in getting Crawford's youngest son, Kevin, a scholarship. Kevin loved basketball too, and was an enthusiastic player. But he wasn't quite good enough for college ball. With Foster's help, he became team manager. He loved the job and was good at it, and his father was proud of his participation.

Crawford introduced Allen to Foster, and the three of them found common interests that roused pleasure in each other's company. They played golf and attended sporting events. They liked getting together for Mexican food and an occasional margarita, although none of the three was a heavy drinker. They went to Vegas together. Crawford's old friend Dean Harrell would set them up with rooms at the Dunes and occasionally join them for golf.

But the traits most common to the three men were their appetites for fun and their mutual quest to live life well. They laughed together easily and fell into comfort that only the depth of sincere friendship can bring.

The sheriff's race had been a difficult loss. To Crawford, it was the World Series, Super Bowl and Heavyweight Championship all in one. He was broke, and heavily in debt. And his career was over, at least temporarily, maybe for good. It was a time when people need support: family, friends, religion. Sharing a burden almost always makes it more manageable.

That wasn't Crawford's way. To tell someone else his problems would be to admit weakness. It's okay to ask favors of friends—that's different, so long as you don't have to tell how you feel, that you're hurting, that you're worried or afraid.

To Crawford, when a man becomes a husband and father, he's required to accept responsibility. It's his obligation. To burden others, especially his family, with his own problems would make him less a man. Their well-being, their happiness, their health, the very air they breathe, is ultimately the responsibility of the father-husband. It is his lot to persist in silence.

Much of the support Crawford had gotten during the sheriff's race was union support, and L. G. Moore was largely the man responsible. He was also the one who came through afterwards. Moore proved to be an influential friend. He was a member of the Texas Board of Amusement Games, as well as an officer of the local chapter of the Operating Engineer's Union. At Moore's suggestion, Crawford applied to the state of Texas for an investigator's position after he failed in his bid for sheriff, but months after the election the job still hadn't materialized. He had to be licensed and his application approved by the board. Moreover, Moore explained, there had to be an opening. Crawford could see that this position would not come as simply as his earlier law enforcement jobs. He was duly worried.

Then came a welcome phone call. Moore told Crawford to be at the operator's union hall the following morning.

Crawford didn't catch on at first. "Why do I need to go down there?"

"You want a job, don't you?" Moore was direct. "Just be there," he said. "And don't ask a lot of questions."

The union hall rang with the hack of long-time smokers. Their stares followed Crawford as he searched the crowd for Moore. Workers milled around in groups of three or four, bored, but at the same time not anxious to be called up. The worn tile floor showed aged scuffmarks and coffee stains. The men frowned under bare fluorescent bulbs and Crawford saw their faces, brown and weathered from lifetimes of outside work. They looked angry.

As Crawford worked his way through the groups, their looks made him wonder if they knew why he was here. Could they know he was about to take a job that one of them should rightly have? He decided it didn't matter—a man has to feed his family.

Moore found Crawford and pulled him by the arm into one of the side offices. There were papers to sign, forms to fill out. They went to another room for photographs. The workers' eyes followed him still. They drilled into his back, filling him with guilt.

Crawford was told that his license and ID tag would be ready in a few days. For now they issued a temporary tag. It read *Hilton Lewis Crawford, Licensed Operating Engineer.*

Moore gave him directions to the job site. It was the new Gulf States facility under construction at Bridge City. It was Crawford's responsibility to start and shut down the welding generators at the beginning and end of each shift and when they broke for lunch. To start the generators, he needed to push a button. It was a big red button, the size of a man's fist. He used his palm, he pushed, and his job was done. For the rest of the workday he sat and watched back-hoe and crane operators move and reposition earth. And he watched the welders guiding handfuls of mesmerizing brilliance from behind their metal masks.

"You'll need to show up by seven," Moore said. "They can't start work until you get there—union rules. Don't forget to wear your hard hat."

On the job there were no more angry looks. The other workers hardly noticed him. Nonetheless, it didn't erase the guilt, and it accented the boredom. But Crawford needed the job—it paid $14 an hour. He continued to work for several months but made up his mind to leave as soon as an opportunity came.

Moore called again. There was another job available. This one sounded more promising: an inspector's position with the Amusement

Game Commission. Unfortunately, he would be based in Lubbock, clear across Texas. But it would be a much-needed foothold with the state. If he did well, it might develop into something better.

He took the job. It was 1977, and he was still heavy in campaign debt. Renting a small efficiency apartment in Lubbock, he commuted on weekends rather than uproot his family. His future was still uncertain. Neither he nor Connie was happy with the arrangement, but they agreed it was best, at least for now.

With no formal training, Crawford was given forms and allotted a territory. His job was to verify each permit, to make sure that each was valid and the tax stamp was up to date. At the time, video games and pinball machines were a growing phenomenon. Game rooms were already prolific and increasing with regularity.

Crawford was anxious to do well. He theorized that if he spent most of his time in game rooms, rather than seeking out locations like convenience stores that had only two or three machines, he could get more done in a shorter time period. Plotting the locations of amusement game permits on a city map, he focused his attention on the areas of greatest concentration. He used his time efficiently and worked long hours. His first group of reports documented almost 300 machines,a very respectable first week, he thought.

The reports were sent on Friday. On Wednesday of the following week he got an urgent call. He knew the voice—it was an official with the Amusement Game Commission, one he had interviewed with. The call was brief. "We need to talk to you today. We're only in town for about an hour, so meet us at the airport."

Why the urgency? he wondered? *What did I do wrong? Did I foul up the report?*

He had erred, but not in the way he thought. The official complimented him on his volume of work and handed the forms back to him. "You can't," he explained. "turn in this much work in one week. Our staff can't handle it."

"And even if they could," the second man said. "There're other considerations. We have to think about our budget. If output increased this much, it would kill any chance for a budget increase. You'll need to rework your reports. Send us only about thirty or forty each week."

"Thirty or forty? Sometimes there're more machines than that in one location—what'll I do for the rest of the week?"

"We don't care. We consider this to be a reasonable workload. You're not expected to do more. In fact, we're *tellin'* you not to do more."

"But what about this week? Whatta I do the rest of this week?"

"It doesn't matter. Just rework the reports and send them in weekly, like we asked."

The first man spoke again. "Here's an idea. You live in Beaumont. Why don't you go home for a while? Be with your family. Just make sure the reports are sent in every week."

Crawford began his first vacation during his second week on the job. It worked out well. With all the spare time he was able to take a second job. Over the next several months he managed to reduce his campaign debt substantially.

V

In order to prepare for the video-taped version of his confession, Crawford was led into a separate room, where his attorney, Special Agent Jones, and Sheriff Williams were already seated. It was an emotional time. Crawford was sobbing and visibly shaking. Adams had already told the officers that McKay was dead. Someone suggested drawing a map to the location of the body. Crawford tried, but he was trembling too badly. Jones took the pad and did most of the drawing. Crawford could hardly talk. He gave instructions as best he could.

After once again being read his rights, Crawford signed a statement that said, among other things: "I understand and know what I am doing. No promises or threats of any kind have been made against me. And no pressure or coercion of any kind has been used against me." *This will end it now. It will all be over once it's told.* Tired and emotionally distraught, he gave a rambling two-hour description of the crime. Monitoring the taped confession and directing questions were FBI Agents Jones and Wargo and Detective Ervin. Attorney Adams was also present.

Crawford told of meeting Remington and how the kidnapping plot was conceived. He gave details as best he could. He tried to sound thorough and cohesive. However, his confusion became apparent when he asked what day it was. "What's today? Tuesday?"

"Today is Sunday," one of the agents said.

Crawford continued to explain their movements up to and including McKay's murder. Agents listened and attempted to clarify his answers: "Where was he standing? Was he struggling? What color was the car? How was he dressed? Did you notice anything else?" Often the agents' response was "uh-huh" or "okay," meaning simply that he should continue.

Around 3 a.m. the session was ended. Crawford was returned to his cell. *It is told—it's over—the weight is lifted.* Sleep came almost instantly.

VI

By 1993 Crawford had begun gambling heavily and the year passed quickly, as years tend to do when one learns to live for the rush. Crawford's habits and attitudes remained unchanged. Like many who gamble and beat the odds as he did in the beginning, he rationalized his losses: *I was just running unlucky—I will win next time.* But as predictable as gambler's logic, so too is the momentum of debt. Interest dollars on credit cards and bank loans collect and swell like a free-rolling snowball, gathering mass with motion.

Crawford managed his debt as best he could, moving it from one credit account to another, paying only the interest on bank loans and borrowing money on credit cards in order to pay it. By early 1994 his indebtedness had reached unmanageable limits. He needed a respite that could come only with a large cash infusion. A big win would do it, but it wasn't happening—things just were not going his way. Nonetheless, as one of his gambler friends said, "Money don't really mean nothin'—it's just something we use. Hell, if I run a little short, I just figure a way to get some more." The statement was made after his friend had just lost $40,000 at the crap table. Crawford remembered its casualness.

Crawford had done it before, figured a way to get more. The insurance scheme had worked once, there was no reason it wouldn't work again. This time, though, he asked his friend, Billy Allen, for help. Lately, Connie had been putting her jewelry in the trunk of her Cadillac for safekeeping whenever the maid came. She always parked in the school lot. Allen, using a key supplied by Crawford, took the car while she was teaching. They timed the theft so that she wouldn't discover the loss before Allen had time to safely store it in one of his rental units. Ironically, the jewelry Crawford reported stolen included all the same items claimed on the earlier loss. The scam netted him $55,000. It was enough to see him through this temporary crisis, enough to make the interest payments and keep up the façade for a while.

Billy Allen had become Crawford's closest friend. He admired Allen for the way he made life work for himself. He was happy and confident, and he knew how to seize opportunity whenever it was offered. He was a gambler, but one who had learned to scoff at losses. If one is smart enough to play the odds and take advantage of situations, he'll be a winner in the long run.

Allen was the one who introduced Crawford to the sport of horseracing with the scam they pulled together involving Off to the Races at Sam Houston Race Park's inaugural season. After Allen lost his racing privileges for the state of Louisiana, he had been ordered to sell the horse. Officially, ownership of Off to the Races transferred several times, yet Allen managed to maintain behind-the-scenes control.

"I'll take care of everything," he told Crawford. "I'll arrange for the horse to be bought in your name. You've never had a case against you so you can run the horse in Texas. Nobody'll ever think nothin' about it. He'll go off at a helluva price. We'll make some good money off him, and you'll get a good horse outta the deal. I'm tellin' you, Hilton, the horse can run."

With a handshake between friends Crawford suddenly became a racehorse owner. He knew nothing about the business or care of racehorses. Not form, nor lineage, nor which strategy a jockey should use. But he knew people, and he knew gambling. He knew he could trust Billy Allen.

Off to the Races was entered to run on the inaugural weekend at Sam Houston. Crawford and his youngest son, Kevin, showed up early at the track. He could feel the excitement coming—like a ballgame, only more intense. As a racehorse owner, he was both fan and player.

The added ingredient of gambling, risk and reward, accented already elevated adrenalin.

Allen had warned Crawford to be careful of his bets, not to be too obvious. "Take this," Crawford told Kevin, handing him a wad of cash, around $1000. "I want you to go to another floor and bet it on our horse."

Crawford, by himself, went to the $10 window. "Gimme $20 across," he said, and settled in to watch his horse.

It happened suddenly. Observers said they drove right up to the front doors, a suburban filled with men in cheap dark suits and old-fashioned haircuts. They split up, some going toward the paddock area, others to the stands. Crawford was pointed out to them.

Two of the men flashed their Identification—Texas Racing Commission. "You Hilton Crawford, owner of Off to the Races?"

Crawford reacted with polite indifference. "That's right."

"You know these men?" They showed pictures of Billy Allen and his brother.

"No. Why? What did they do?"

"Never mind. Lessee your tickets for this race."

"Huh?"

"Your tickets. We want to see your wagers."

Hilton showed them the pari-mutuel tickets.

"No, we want to see them all. Everything you bet on this race."

"That's it," he said. "That's all of'm." He voluntarily turned his pockets inside out.

"Twenty across? Sixty dollars is all you bet? Don't you think your horse is gonna win?"

"Well, hell, I don't know what'll happen. It's a horse race."

The men looked at each other and handed the tickets back. "Thanks, Mr. Crawford. Good luck in the race."

Crawford smiled. He would still have to be careful. They would probably watch him collect his winnings.

There is something about thoroughbred horses, their nervous energy and sleek musculature. They're more aerodynamic than quarter horses. They seem to have more determination, more stamina, more heart. Quarter horses run shorter distances. They often just run a straight line, no curves or complexities—it just becomes a contest to see which horse can run the fastest on any given day. But with thoroughbreds there has to be a game plan. Distance and position have to be considered. Thoroughbreds have to be able to respond to the jockey. They have to be ready to give the extra effort when he asks for it.

Crawford had been to racetracks and had made some small bets, but before Off to the Races he never had more than a passing interest. With the Billy Allen scheme came ownership, and that was altogether different. As an owner, he became the one ultimately responsible for the horse's success. He was the one who managed and made decisions that influenced the horse's winning potential. That day in 1994, when Off to the Races crossed the finish line first and was led into the winner's circle, when Crawford stood next to him as the cameras flashed and moved his hand across the horse's sweating neck, he felt the beat of a winner's heart. It mirrored his own.

Owning and racing horses quenched a need in Crawford, almost as if he had been looking for something his whole life and finally found it. The horses' pounding determination reminded him of his athletic younger days. And there was the gamble, the rush that comes with risk when adrenaline pumps a sort of satisfaction into a life long dulled through lack of physical competition. Texas' newly legalized pari-mutuel betting added convenience to Crawford's compulsive instincts. He was drawn to the betting windows as Aeneid was drawn to the sun, and his fall was inevitable.

Joe Duhon was Crawford's trainer, a serious young man whose family Crawford had known from his Beaumont years. He knew horses. He could see potential in an unknown animal, and he knew how to work horses to maximize their abilities. He became Crawford's teacher and confidant, sharing his insights about workout times and track conditions, and explaining why horses won or lost. (He would later testify at Crawford's trial, repeating a Crawford hyperbole, "I'll get your money, Joe, if I have to go out and kill somebody for it." Duhon understood the context and knew that it was just a figure of speech. He never expected that Crawford would literally *kill someone* in order to pay past-due training bills.)

Duhon and Allen became Crawford's guides to the glamorous and sometimes shady world of horse racing. They offered the benefit of their influence and contact. Unlike Allen, neither Crawford nor Duhon had the taint of prior misdeeds and thus were able to compete in both Texas and Louisiana tracks. Within weeks Off to the Races had been entered in a full racing schedule in both states.

The horse was a consistent winner, nine wins in fourteen starts. But even with that kind of record, profit was elusive. The care and maintenance of racehorses is expensive. There are entry fees, veterinarian fees, training and stabling costs. Owners, even the ones who know the business well, often have a difficult time showing a profit.

Sometimes, through Allen, Duhon or one of their associates, Crawford would get insider information. Maybe the fix would be in on a race, or maybe they simply knew of a horse that was rounding to form. If the information was reliable, it usually meant a windfall. Crawford would bet the horse to win, but the real money was made on exactas and trifectas, combining the horse that was expected to win with others that were likely to run second and third. The odds on these types of bets are sometimes phenomenal, and the tips, the ones that come from trusted sources, could mean a win of several hundred dollars on a single race. But then there were all the races in between.

VII

Early in 1978 the state investigator job Crawford had been waiting for came through. He went to work for the Texas State Board of Licensed Private Investigators and Private Security Firms. His duties were to police the operation of licensed individuals and security companies. He was based in Houston and responsible for Southeastern Texas.

Initially, he moved to an apartment in the Greenspoint area. The arrangement was similar to the one they had when he worked in Lubbock. He went home on the weekends. Only now he was much closer, just a couple of hours' drive.

Crawford was anxious for his family to be together again in a permanent location, but he didn't want to raise his boys in Houston. He wanted a close-knit community where people knew each other, like the place where he grew up. The little town of Conroe, thirty miles north of Houston, seemed perfect. He found a house on North Rivershire, and in March he and the boys moved in. Connie stayed behind only long enough to finish out the school year.

They settled quickly into the community. The boys were nine and thirteen, difficult ages to adjust to a new town, but Hilton and Connie were loving parents. They made the transition as painless as possible by spending much of their free time together as a family. Hilton began his volunteer work again, coaching pony league, little league, and boys' basketball. It didn't matter whether or not his boys were on the team, he coached where he was needed, but he always found extra time to help the teams his sons were assigned to.

Connie got a job with the Conroe School District teaching first grade at the new C.E. Rice Elementary. It was there she met Paulette Everett, who taught in the classroom just across the hall. They made friends easily and remained close for years—until McKay's murder.

The Crawfords began attending Sacred Heart Catholic Church almost as soon as they arrived. Church activities were mainly in Connie's realm. She gracefully guided the family into Conroe's Catholic community, where they were warmly received.

Life in Conroe was pleasant for the family. But for Crawford there was no recognition, no name identity, no familiar feeling of a grateful community. These remained in the past. He was no longer unique, an odd feeling for Crawford. His image in this community was different and, gradually, his values changed as well. Financial independence was becoming an important measure of his self-worth. He began to see himself as he imagined others saw him, looking seldom beyond cars, clothes, home, lifestyle. These were now the criteria by which he came to judge himself. They became his identity.

In 1979 Crawford made the decision to go into private industry. He went to work for Billy Stevens, owner of Security Guard Services, one of the companies he regularly inspected for the state. The company specialized in industrial security—supplying guards for plants, office buildings, and the like. His new job title was supervisor, and as such was in charge of a limited group of accounts. He was responsible for the hiring, training and scheduling at each location. But his primary responsibility, the function upon which his job depended, was keeping the customers happy. That is to say, whether the firm was as large as Louisiana-Pacific, or as small as an independent East Texas sawmill, he had to satisfy the person who wrote the checks—a basic business concept.

To this end, Crawford was well suited. He made sure to take larger clients out to lunch every two or three weeks and call them every day, just to see if there were any problems. But he usually knew the answer before the question. His first duty, every morning, was to check the event reports from the previous night and day. That way he was on top of potential problems, in many cases, even before management of the target company. What business could be unhappy with a security service that knew of complaints even before they were reported?

Marvin Keller saw his potential immediately. Keller was Crawford's immediate supervisor and the man responsible for bringing Crawford to Security Guard Services. They became close friends. (Keller would remain supportive, even during the investigation and indictment. When contacted by the *Conroe Courier*, he stated, "He [Crawford] loved his family very much. He kept his problems to himself." The Crawford he knew could not have been guilty.)

For the Crawfords, with Hilton settled into a well-paying job in private industry and Connie teaching school, life for the next few years was normal—church, community functions, golf on the weekends—typical suburban lifestyles. Of course, for Hilton there was an occasional trip to Vegas as well.

One of the friends Crawford soon made on the Conroe golf courses was Sam Petro. Overweight and overbearing, Sam was the kind of person people seldom say no to. He owned and operated a successful produce distribution company out of Houston, but his talent was sales, talking people into doing, saying, buying, things they would never otherwise consider. In Crawford's case it was a restaurant partnership.

There were doubts, however. Crawford had seen Petro cheat on the golf course and slow-pay gambling debts. There's not a lot of shame in a man betting more than he can afford to lose on a given weekend, it could happen to anyone who loved sports. But to shave strokes during a friendly golf game, or slyly kick his ball to a better lie—those were sure signs of flawed character. He saw it even in tournament play. It was embarrassing.

But Petro was a good salesman. He countered all Crawford's objections. "Experience? To run a restaurant? We don't need experience. We'll hire people with experience. You don't worry. I'll take care of it."

"Money? We don't need money. We incorporate. We borrow the money we need. We rent the building. We lease the equipment. You don't worry. I'll take care of it."

"A good location is what we need and we've got that. The new center at the loop and I-45. Damn! Just look at the traffic! I've got the lease already nailed down. You don't worry. It's all taken care of."

Crawford finally agreed to meet with the banker. He didn't really think they could get a loan, not for the $125,000 they asked for, but Petro convinced him to at least join him in making the application.

The banker's name was Bob Izzo. At first he said no.

"Too much risk," he said. "The loan committee doesn't really like us to do these kinds of deals."

Petro never flinched.

"There's no risk. This is gonna to be a nice restaurant, the kind Conroe needs. Great wine list. Gourmet food. There's nothing else like it in town."

Petro sensed the banker's interest.

"And here's what we're gonna do for you. We like your name. You tell us we can use it and that's what we'll call the restaurant. IZZO'S ITALIAN RESTAURANT, in big neon letters, right over the door."

The banker leaned forward.

"Anytime you want, come in, bring three or four friends, everything's comp. You pay for nothing."

The banker grinned.

"In fact, we'll even act like we work for you. We'll come to your table, say hello, Mr. Izzo, good evening, Mr. Izzo, how nice to see you, Mr. Izzo. We'll spread out the napkin and put it in your lap, like this. We'll bring your favorite wine. Hell, it'll be even better than owning the place!"

They laughed.

Crawford and Petro left with a commitment for $125,000 in operating capital—and a name for the restaurant.

Izzo's was indeed one of the nicest places to eat in Conroe. Petro had contacts through his produce business who helped with the design and equipment. And they found a good chef. The place was packed almost every night. On Friday and Saturday there was often a two-hour wait.

Petro enjoyed the role of host. He dressed loudly, red coats with yellow ties, unforgettable combinations. He talked to customers and mingled. And Bob Izzo wasn't the only one who got complimentary meals. It seemed to Crawford that the string of Petro's friends was never ending. Nonetheless, the restaurant enjoyed a healthy volume—it looked as if it would be a success.

But volume means little without good management. At first they did okay. They weren't getting rich, but the business was profitable. Then food costs began to grow and deposits began to shrink, one of the first indications of theft. Crawford felt sure Petro was helping himself to a little extra cash. But he did own the restaurant, or at least half of it.

Petro began taking draws as well. He wrote checks, $1000, sometimes $1500. He would write two checks, in equal amounts, one to Crawford and one to himself. If Crawford suggested they couldn't afford to take any money out of the business, Petro countered with, "I'm takin' mine. I need it. You can leave yours in if you want to."

In the third year of operation they fell months behind in payroll taxes. They could no longer meet their notes. In 1985, Izzo's was closed and both men filed bankruptcy.

(Ironically, the restaurant was in the same shopping center used for a meeting a decade later with another injudiciously chosen partner. It was where Crawford picked up R.L. Remington on their way to kidnap McKay Everett.)

VIII

Several hours after his first taped confession, Crawford was again taken from his cell to the interview room. "We've got some problems," he was told. "There are some questions about your first statement. We just need to straighten a few things out."

There was no mention of the video recorder. Crawford and Adams were seated first. The recorder was already running as attorney and client spoke privately. The tape would later have to be edited before it could be presented to a jury.

Agents told Crawford about possible inconsistencies in his story. In addition, there was an omission that Crawford himself volunteered. They allowed him to talk first. He explained how he hadn't thought to buy gas ahead of time and his car was almost on empty. He told how they "filled up at the Diamond Shamrock" after McKay was abducted.

Agents seemed incredulous. "You were at the Diamond Shamrock station with McKay in the trunk?" Crawford insisted that it had happened just as he said.

The first irregularity agents mentioned was that the witness, Bill Kahn, who saw the car backing out as he was taking out the trash, noticed no sign of commotion at the Everett house. According to Crawford's testimony, McKay had been kicking and struggling. "How does he not see that?" one of the agents asked.

"I have no idea." It seemed obvious that agents already thought he had done it alone. *Don't they realize that McKay would have struggled, no matter who put him in the trunk?* The only real explanation was that Mr. Kahn simply did not notice what was happening across the street.

Agents must have already doubted the existence of R. L. Remington, even at this early stage. If this was indeed the case—if the FBI's theory was that Crawford acted alone—logic dictates that for the next few weeks, as long as the case remained open, at least as much effort would be expended attempting to prove this theory as would be spent actually searching for the R. L. Remington character they already believed to be nonexistent. In fact, all of the questions agents asked during the second interview were aimed at discrediting Crawford's claim of the other man's involvement.

The next discrepancy agents referred to was Crawford's statement that the man in the Cadillac was waiting on the freeway. An agent explained: "I've tried to hook up with people before. This car is sitting for how . . . God knows how long on the side of the road on I-10 and you guys meet this car perfectly, perfect timing."

"Uh-huh." *Don't they know that the guy in the burgundy Cadillac is probably the one who brought Remington to Conroe? Don't they realize how likely it is that he waited to see if Remington was going to be picked up before he left—might have even followed them!* Crawford told them he hadn't noticed the license number. In the previous interview, however, he had mentioned that he recalled seeing a "Thibodaux Motors" decal.

Next they wanted to know about the gun. They implied that only Crawford's prints were on it and wanted to know why Remington let him keep it. They asked if Remington was wearing gloves. By this time the interview had deteriorated to such a point that agents were becoming antagonistic. It became interrogation rather than interview.

"He didn't have no gloves," Crawford said.

"So if only your prints are on it?"

"Well that's . . . I mean. I'm not going to sit here and argue. That's what happened."

"No. We're not arguing here. We're just telling you why we have a problem."

Adams intervened: "This is arguing."

Another question was why Remington had let Crawford remain alive. "You watched a murder, and some guy you don't even know is going to let you leave?"

Crawford had no ready answer. He told of threats made on his family. However, during interviews held after his conviction, he admitted that the threats were embellished so officers would believe him. He claimed that the threats were actually only implied. Nonetheless, it is likely that Crawford felt a serious concern for himself and his family. What is even more likely, though, is that Remington simply considered him an accomplice. As such, there would be little practical reason to kill him. Disposing of the additional body and vehicle would have presented further difficulties. Also, when and if the bodies were found, investigators would know beyond a doubt that someone else had been involved. The FBI's full focus would be on him, and he had no way of knowing just how much information Crawford had actually shared with Flores. It was better for Remington to let Crawford live.

The final exchange in the interview involved the question of whose prints Crawford thought should be on the gun. He was trying to explain when one of the agents interrupted him.

"You got all kinds . . .," Crawford said.

"Got you, all right."

Based on the map and directions Crawford supplied, agents were able to direct officials in Louisiana to the location of McKay's body. In the early morning hours of Sunday, September 17th, likely before

Crawford was finished giving his first official statement, Detective Marcus Guidry of St. Martin Parish Sheriff's Department followed the directions to the desolate swampy area known as Whisky Bay. With his windows down he recognized the odor of decaying human flesh as soon as he left the Interstate. He parked in the middle of a shell road close to where the smell was strongest.

It was merely coincidence that Deputy Jerry Stassi of the Iberville Parish Sheriff's Department spotted Guidry's unmarked Camero and decided to check it as a suspicious vehicle. Guidry identified himself and explained his purpose in the remote area. Stassi then joined him in the search. They followed the smell through the fence and several yards off the right-of-way. Weeds were dense and three to four feet tall. In the beams of their flashlights they found what seemed to be a sort of depression in the weeds, as if someone had recently walked through them. They moved forward slowly, raking the area with their lights, so as not to blunder onto the body and compromise the scene. Stassi was first to see the body.

"Over here—I got something." Through the weeds he could make out the lower half of a corpse. He could see jean-clad legs.

Guidry aimed his flashlight at the same spot. He could see the blue jeans and what looked like white socks below them. They were no more than fifty feet away. A possum was feeding on the body. They waved their lights and it scurried away.

The two officers secured the area and radioed for crime-scene investigators. The first of many began to arrive in about twenty minutes. They and others like them would be there searching for evidence for the next several days. Word was sent back to Conroe that the body had been found. It was exactly where Crawford had said it would be.

It had been a difficult five days for Agents Wargo and Jones. They had worked tirelessly to bring McKay home and, in the process, had come to feel the grief of those who loved him.

Part 5: Remington

I

Crawford had been scarcely bothered by the failure of Izzo's restaurant. The debt had been settled by bankruptcy and, since they had incorporated, it reflected little on his personal credit. By 1985 his lifestyle was already beyond his means if he had needed to rely on salary alone. But during this time he was making extra money betting sports and laying off bets for Butch Holmes. He had convinced himself of his earning power. Occasionally, he worried about how he would meet all his financial obligations, but he always managed to come through, just like he came through in the clutch ballgames back in high school.

His first over-commitment had been buying the house on South Rivershire a couple of years after they moved to Conroe. It was nicer than the one they lived in on North Rivershire, which had also cost more than they could really afford. But Connie wanted the house. He could feel her excitement whenever they looked at it, or even talked about it. He had to buy it for her.

The thought of obligating himself again for a payment that would stretch family resources every month was frightening. It was almost like doing something morally disagreeable. But buying the house for Connie was important to him. He'd find a way to make the payments. He would do whatever it took.

And so he did. It was a little difficult at first. But living beyond his primary means was easier than he thought. There had only been a few times, a half-dozen at most, when he had trouble with the payments, when he had to juggle payments. In this manner he convinced himself that he could depend on his own ingenuity.

During Izzo's operation he took draws whenever Petro did. But

Crawford never depended on this money to meet his obligations. In fact, by this time he worried little—money was only the system used to fill life's scorecard. He could overcome an occasional bad round. The restaurant's closing meant almost nothing, only a slight glitch.

A 1986 change in ownership of the security company he was employed by was more bothersome. California Plant Protection, CPP, had bought out Security Guard Services some years earlier, but the changeover was hardly felt. The employees were all retained; there was no change in management or policy; chain of command was the same; everything was left as it was. The California company was happy with profits and opted not to try and improve something that was already working well.

But in 1986 CPP bought the nationwide Pinkerton Security Company. In order to take advantage of national name recognition, CPP chose to convert to Pinkerton Security. And, in spite of the fact that local employees and management was retained, Crawford's company fell under the control of Pinkerton's corporate policy and supervision.

The once small company, Security Guard Services, was now part of a large corporation. Employees had to adjust to a more rigid on-the-job atmosphere. Uniforms were changed, including those of the supervisors. No longer would Crawford go to work in golf shirts—it was strictly coat and tie. And there were the inevitable myriad reports, checks and balances. Simply showing profit was not enough—it needed to be maximized.

It was a difficult change for Crawford. Corporate culture was something of which he was totally unfamiliar. But he adapted. Keller was still his boss. There were tighter limits on his expense account, but he was still expected to visit clients, take them to lunch, etc.

However, the change was tolerated only until the directive for a salary cut to the employees came through. They already had what he considered low-paying jobs. Many were elderly, retired from other careers. Some were single parents, barely getting by. It seemed unthinkable to tell them they would be earning less. Thus, in spite of their past history, Crawford was interested when Sam Petro told him his uncle owned a security service and wanted to talk.

After Izzo's closed, Petro had come to Crawford for a loan. The bank had called in a second lien, and he was going to lose his house.

As was often the case, sympathy clouded Crawford's judgment. He loaned Petro $6000, to be repaid in monthly installments of around $400. Getting him to pay the monthly note was always a challenge. Crawford was uncomfortable as a collector, especially with a friend. He strongly resented Petro for making him ask for the payments. Even so, he was angry enough with Pinkerton to listen when Petro told him about Charles Kalil, his uncle. A meeting was set at Kalil's Houston office on Airline Drive, close to the produce center.

There's something exciting about an open-air market on a crisp fall morning. Vendors display their products—melons, tomatoes, green peppers—and trim leaves and tilt boxes while buyers walk the aisles and decide which lettuce is greenest, and which potatoes have been above ground the shortest time. Prices are set, bargained for, and set again. The energy comes from commerce in its purest form: buyers and sellers together, face-to-face, motivated and electric.

Kalil knew the market, its character, and its energy. He met Crawford outside and put his foot on a car bumper. He carried a yellow legal pad.

"Here's what we'll do," he said. "We're going to make money."

He drew a line on the tablet. "See this line? This is our first million." With a flourish he made a check mark over the line.

"See this next line? It's our second million." He checked each line and looked at Crawford—eye contact—face-to-face.

"And this line is our third million."

He offered solid reasoning. Crawford was to leave Pinkerton and bring with him his customers. Kalil owned two security licenses; Crawford was to be a partner in one of them. He would own 48% of the company, while Kalil retained 52%.

"This line? This is our fourth million."

Kalil told Crawford not to worry about money. He said he owned lots of companies. He would divert whatever operating capital they needed.

"See here? This'll be our fifth million."

They shook hands. The new company was called State Security.

"This other line? This is our sixth million. This is where we decide. We either sell the business—or go on to the next page."

II

After the inaugural season in Houston, Off to the Races ran frequently at Louisiana Downs in Shreveport. It was convenient for Crawford since one of his major clients, Louisiana Pacific, had several plants in eastern Texas. He could time his trips to take care of any weekly business on the way. From the easternmost plants it was only another hour or so to Shreveport. He often took Connie and usually stayed the weekend, leaving after Sunday's matinee race card.

He not only went to Louisiana Downs, but he sometimes got a tip on a horse running at Jefferson Downs in New Orleans or Oaklawn Park in Hot Springs. All were within reasonable driving distance. It was during a weekend trip to Shreveport, however, that he met a man he came to know as R. L. Remington.

It was late spring or early summer, and Off to the Races was running. Connie's school year had not yet ended, but Crawford had convinced her to come along anyway. Traffic had been heavy coming into the track, and they were running a little late. Crawford stopped in the valet area and thrust a five-dollar bill in the direction of a young man. It disappeared instantly, sucked up like he had fed it into one of the video poker machines lining the walls in Louisiana truck stops. In its place was a numbered stub. There was only the action—no words were exchanged.

Crawford held Connie's arm as they moved toward the entry gate. Surrounding them were other valet customers, bejeweled women with stiffly-coiffured hair-dos and their spouses—the track's high rollers, men carrying wads of money in their front pockets. They were the ones who had learned to enjoy life and let it work for them, rather than spend it punching the clock for a weekly paycheck. Now he was one of them. He felt vital and alive.

It was close to race time, only twenty minutes till post. There wasn't enough time to study the past performances—that is, to do it right, consider all the facts. He would have to get them seated, making sure Connie was comfortable, then he could look at *The Racing Form*. He would only have time to compare speed. There wasn't time to consider class, breeding, form, jockey, and all the other necessary ingredients that go into choosing the winning horse. The most important thing was to get a bet down before race time.

Crawford ordered a pitcher of iced tea and scanned the form.

He quickly eliminated the favorites. There was no logic in picking an even-money shot in a twelve-horse race—that was a sucker bet. He focused only on the horses that he felt had a real chance of winning and, of those, chose the two with the longest odds. He looked quickly at the second race as well and picked a couple of horses to box in the daily double.

He turned for a moment at the top of the stairs and watched the changing tote board numbers before joining a group of last-minute players waiting in line to bet. Others hurried in all directions, their glazed expressions indifferent to fellow players. They bobbed along, hoping for the fastest moving line. To be shut out at the window was even worse than losing.

"The horses are in the starting gate." The announcement came just as Crawford finished his wagers. As an afterthought he added, "And give me an exacta wheel with the six horse on top." Even as he peeled the hundred dollar bill and three twenties from the weekend's bankroll, he heard the race being called.

"Annnd—they're off!" returned the throaty voice with its artificially layered excitement. "Taking the early lead is . . . ." He had heard the singsong cadence many times, but he never listened to the words, only sensed their meaning. When the excitement of a race is at its peak, it's difficult to focus on more than the visual. As the horses rounded the second turn, he found his jockey's colors and tried to make out his horse's movements. It had dropped to fifth, but was still only four lengths off the lead, with good enough position, especially for a strong closer.

As he watched, the familiar excitement rose, alive and brash. Passing the third turn, his horse gained ground to fourth, about three lengths out. Crowd noise increased, changing from clamor to roar. It would become louder still, growing steadily until the horses rounded the last turn and headed into the stretch. Then, until they crossed the finish line, it would stay at a thunderous volume.

"Number five—now—do it now!" someone screamed. Crawford's horse was moving up on the outside, but number five was moving too, and he had the rail.

Crawford could no longer suppress the urge to shout. "Push him! Push him, damn it!" But going outside had cost too much ground—number five pulled away at the wire.

He was always emotionally drained after a race. But this was only one loss. There was a long program ahead and Off to the Races was running in the ninth.

Connie was casually sipping iced tea when he returned to the table. "I didn't know which horse to root for. Did you win?"

"Nope. He got a bad start. Came in second. Let's get something to eat." Crawford didn't usually disclose the amounts he lost, or if asked, he would lie. He didn't consider himself deceitful. He just wanted to spare Connie's feelings. She didn't need to hear about the losses. He only wanted her to be happy.

He sorted through his losing tickets in the off-chance that the cashier had mistakenly added the number five horse to one of his combinations. There was no such lucky coincidence, and his attention returned to The Racing Form. It was time to figure the second race. He was more deliberate on this one.

III

After agreeing to Kalil's terms, the transition from employee to company owner was relatively easy. Kalil stayed in the background, allowing his new partner complete freedom in converting accounts and employees. Crawford talked with the people who ran his larger accounts. His biggest was Louisiana Pacific, a large holder of Texas timberlands and processing plants in the state's eastern regions. Another key client was a downtown office building that housed Houston Metro. For the most part they committed to following him. He was diligent in taking care of problems or addressing any special needs they might have. And he entertained them well: with lunches, afternoon golf games, even guided fishing trips at Amistad Reservoir, hundreds of miles away. His customer contacts were treated like personal friends. Who wouldn't follow a friend?

Crawford also treated his employees well. He spoke with them individually, asking each to join him in his new company. None refused. After all, he was the one they looked to as their "boss." He was the one who helped with their problems and saw to it that the paychecks were delivered on time. He made them laugh with his unceasing humor. Sometimes, he bought washer and dryer sets for the more needy of them through his friend, John Powell at Conn's Appliances, and gave them to employees that needed help. He even co-signed an occasional car loan. He made their jobs bearable. And what had Pinkerton done for them but cut their salaries? It wasn't a hard sell.

His employees trusted him. He would guide them to a better life. He was their shepherd, a role he was comfortable in. They were almost like family to him, and a man doesn't fail his own.

But Billy Stevens, the prior owner of Security Guard Services who remained with the company after Pinkerton took control, was convinced Crawford was making a big mistake. Billy was on the elevator as Crawford left after finishing his last day. "Hilton," he said. "I want the best for you, but I wish you'd reconsider. I've been in this business a long time, and I can tell you now—you ain't gonna make it on your own." It was an ominous warning, one on which Crawford would later reflect.

Early in 1990 Crawford leased office space on 19th street, close to the produce center, and began operations as State Security. He started with an enthusiasm and diligence he hadn't known for years. His days began early, and he often worked well into the night. But his personal habits didn't change much. He still bet on sports and enjoyed golf an afternoon or two each week and still went to Vegas with his friends.

He soon found that the responsibility of operating a business as its owner carries with it a whole new set of problems. In addition to the routine of dealing with customers and employees, and the technical end—actually providing security—he now had to cope with the company's financial side: projections, budgets, cash flow, worrying about how much money was in the bank and how much more he would need to cover payroll. He could no longer make decisions based solely on "employee need" or "customer good will."

These new paradigms were awkward. Perhaps it had been necessary for Pinkerton to cut employee salaries in order to sustain itself, rather than simply to try and increase net profit as he originally thought. But he couldn't accept the concept—to calculate coldly the respective worth of profit versus people was not within his scope. To lay off employees or lessen customer benefits weren't seen by him as viable options. His answer to any cash shortfall or unexpected expense was to increase gross. He saw no alternatives.

Perhaps Kalil, as the controlling partner, recognized this weakness in Crawford. People who accumulate wealth often have keen insight in matters such as these. Whatever the reason, their partnership did not last. Before the year was out Kalil announced that he was selling the business—ironically, back to Pinkerton.

Crawford felt betrayed. He had worked hard, building the company by adding new accounts and making sure they held onto the ones they had. To suddenly have the business sold out from under him wasn't right. There was no fairness in this action, but there was nothing he could do.

"What about my end? What do I get out of the deal?" he asked.

Kalil explained that he had nothing coming, slapping the pocket containing his wallet. "The money to operate this business came from my pocket. You think we started from air? The money came from here, from inside this back pocket . . . and now it's going back into this pocket!"

"You can't do it! You can't sell off my clients. I brought them in. They belong to me." In his mind they were indeed his, his employees and his customers. He was the one who took the midnight phone calls. He did the hiring, the firing, negotiated the contracts, signed the leases. It would seem like selling his friends. "They won't go back to Pinkerton," he argued. "They'll quit! I'll go to work for another company and have them all back, clients and employees, in three months!"

Kalil reviewed his position. Legally he was within his rights, but maybe Crawford had a point, maybe it would be best to find an alternative solution that would keep everyone happy. "Let me think about this, Hilton. I'll get back to you in a few days. I'll let you know."

Crawford didn't know what to do. All he could think of was to let the situation play itself out. After a few days of silence, Kalil was ready to talk.

"Hilton, maybe this isn't so fair to you. You've worked hard, and I don't want all your sweat to go unrewarded. I have decided to let you keep two big accounts, Louisiana Pacific and the Houston Metro building. From these you can build." The accounts were Crawford's most loyal clients—he had brought them from Pinkerton. "This is probably not good business on my part, certainly not anything I have to do. It's just that I want to do right by you. I'll arrange a loan at Northwest Bank for operating capital, so you won't have problems meeting payroll. But in return I have to ask you to do something for me. It's the only way I'll consider doing this. You have to take my nephew in as a partner."

"Who? Sam? Sam Petro?"

"That's right. He's a good man, a thinker, a man who can put deals together. He can make things happen for you. You're friends, and you've worked together before in the restaurant business. This is a good thing, Hilton. It's a good deal for both of you."

Crawford thought it over. Kalil was right about Petro putting deals together. He remembered the restaurant deal, put together from nothing. He had made money, even though they had taken bankruptcy. And the business shouldn't have failed. It had done well at first; it was just managed badly. He had known nothing about restaurant operation, but the security business was a different story. With Crawford himself as the manager, maybe Petro wouldn't be such a bad partner to have.

"I'll have to talk with Sam first. He'll need to understand that it's going to be rough going until we get on our feet. Won't neither of us be able to take any money out of the company. And he's gotta know that I'm runnin' the show!"

"Yeah, sure. He knows these things, I already talked to him. You won't have to worry about Sam—he'll be okay. I'll see he goes along with whatever you want. You don't worry."

IV

After winning a short-paying exacta in the second race, which only allowed him to salvage a portion of what he had wagered, Crawford decided to abandon his handicapping efforts, at least temporarily, and search out a more dependable system, insider information. As an owner, Crawford felt like he was now one of the "in" crowd. Owners, trainers and jockeys often have bits of useful information they're willing to share with others who might reciprocate. He headed for the area overlooking the paddocks.

"Hey, 'migo." The voice, soft and unctuous, came from behind him. It belonged to J. M. Nixon, sometimes called Jam by his friends. He was a long-time horse owner and short-time friend of Crawford. "Ain't that nag a' yours runnin' today?"

Crawford grasped the outstretched hand in his own firm grip. His father had taught him long ago that the depth of a man's worth was reflected in the strength of his grip. Never trust a man with a weak handshake.

"Yeah, Off to the Races is running in the ninth. We're pretty sure he'll be in the money, but he probably won't pay too good. He's favored in the morning line."

"Well, thanks. Maybe I'll use him in a tri-box or something." Then, in keeping with horseplayer etiquette he added, "I don't have anything. Had a horse in today's program but he already ran. If I'd seen you earlier I could have given you the double. He ran out of the five-hole. I had him heavy with the six and seven—made a nice payday."

Crawford remembered the five horse. "Shit! Your horse cost me the race."

"Wish I'd seen you earlier. I'll try and look you up if I hear anything else."

Wish I'd seen you earlier. It wasn't the first time Crawford had heard the phrase. He was beginning to understand. Nixon was like most of the other owners: They didn't give a good Goddamn about Hilton Crawford's misfortune. They shared information when it was convenient and listened to each other's problems, but it was all part of the game. Gamblers, serious ones, don't really care about one another. They listen, but only to feel better *themselves*.

V

To Crawford, his wife's beauty and grace increased with age. He loved doing things for her, pleasing her and seeing her smile. She spent routine days with her first-graders, listening to laughing children and sometimes drying their tears. With children there were no difficult, awkward moments as with adults, never an unpredictable reaction. In her marriage there were often surprises. Crawford saw to it.

Over the course of their union Crawford had become the husband he always wanted to be. He was in part his own father, with a silent strength that could quell any suffering. As a dad himself he felt an extraordinary commitment to maintain financial security, just as his father had done. Second to security came happiness. But to Crawford happiness was only a surface effect: comfort, excitement, entertainment. It was dining out, nice clothes, luxury automobiles, vacations—trappings of an affluent culture. It was winning a ballgame in the final seconds, and knowing the adoration of fans. These were the feelings he wanted for his wife and sons.

His sons, though, couldn't follow his example. They tried, and performed reasonably well, but there was nothing outstanding about their play. In spite of all his attention, and his constant instruction, they were not exceptional ballplayers. They didn't have the drive or the heart. They accepted defeat too easily.

Connie was even less competitive. For her, the real joy of life was in the comfort of her home, knowing nothing would change. The VCR was set to record her favorite soaps, and at night, after a day attending to the needs of six-year-olds, she relaxed to the complex drama of adult relationships. In the plots she saw dilemmas like none she had experienced, nor ever thought she would. Her husband was her support, the one who had replaced her father. He was her wall, as solid and strong as the red bricks and mortar that would later hold him until his execution.

After being sent to Death Row, Crawford exchanged a few letters with a female acquaintance who had known them both in high school. "It's no wonder you two stayed married so many years," she wrote. "You did everything for her. God! How you spoiled her! I know she's having a rough time without you."

Connie accepted her husband's leadership and his lifestyle, and he, in turn, understood that she needed his guidance. He held himself responsible for breaking her routine, for making life fun. Not much of a gambler, she played only cheap slots or went to the two-dollar window at the track, but she liked going with him. She would get excited, maybe scream or jump up and down. He liked her that way.

On January 24, 1991, Connie turned fifty. It was an occasion that called for something special—a celebration of life's half-century mark, together with the friends who had helped live it. The Everetts were among those considered friends. Paulette agreed to help, even volunteering her home for a surprise party.

Crawford enlisted the aid of Connie's sister, still in the Beaumont area, who invited several of her old-time chums. A number of local friends also accepted invitations. He arranged for catering from Jason's Deli, and ordered cases of wine and champagne delivered in advance. Paulette supplied the cake.

The premise he used to facilitate the surprise was that their old friends, Carl and Paulette Everett, had asked them out to dinner to help celebrate her birthday. Paulette took great care to see that everything was done properly. She saw to it that no one parked in the front; there was nothing to tip off the surprise. She greeted the Crawfords and led them into the family room, where the throng, too many to hide, yelled their welcome.

The Everetts were wonderful hosts. Crawford's resentment of Carl over a failed oil well venture had waned. Besides, it never had anything to do with Paulette. He was just grateful they had helped make this day special for Connie. That was the important thing— making Connie happy.

VI

The new firm, with Petro as a partner instead of Kalil, started business early in 1991. Crawford kept the name State Security and continued to office in the same Houston location, Loop 610 North, where the company had moved months earlier. In fact, nothing much changed. There were fewer clients, but the faces that remained were familiar. However, Sam Petro was now coming into the office almost every day. Crawford didn't really care, though, as long as he stayed out of the way and didn't interfere with company operations.

Colleen Hawthorne still ran the office. She had been hired early in the partnership with Kalil. She was the daughter of one of his biggest clients, the building manager of the Houston Metro Building. It seemed like a win-win proposition—she needed a job, and they needed to maintain the client's good will. Crawford later discovered a flaw in this logic.

While he didn't mind Petro's presence in the office, he did feel uneasy about his old restaurant partner's honesty. He soon began to see familiar problems. Petro had been issued a company credit card for expenses—gas, client lunches and such—statements for which reflected questionable charges almost immediately. There were weekend dinners—probably with family, since clients weren't usually entertained on weekends—and personal items, even baby furniture for a new grandchild. There was clothing, and a pair of mountain bikes. Bills that should have been less than a couple of hundred dollars were as high as three thousand. To further problems, Crawford also discovered that Petro had instructed the office manager to pay his personal car note out of company funds. Perhaps a small usage allowance was justified, but not the whole $650 payment. And, it was done without consulting him.

Fewer than three months passed before Crawford realized that the new arrangement was a mistake. He knew he would have to find a way out, soon. But people depended on him—he had made promises; he couldn't just walk away. Thus, he sought out an old acquaintance, Charley Wasco, and told him he wanted to sell. Wasco was a friend who had been in and out of the security business for years and had several connections. By November they had a possible buyer. Crawford was cautiously jubilant.

VII

Losing a close race has a tendency to cause one's mouth to dry. Crawford returned to Connie and a waiting pitcher of iced tea. Even the sight of condensation on the glass had a calming effect. Anyone who has ever lived through the heat of a Texas or Louisiana summer knows the soothing property of iced tea. Like the scent of rain, it foreshadows relief.

Returning to his handicapping, Crawford went winless in the third, but in the fourth collected on a straight-win ticket and an exacta with a payoff big enough to recoup his losses. Nonetheless, the relief was only temporary. In spite of his meticulous critique of the past performances, he was blanked in the next two races—just stupid bad luck. Again he went in search of insider tips.

There were several people looking at the horses in the paddocks, none of whom he recognized. Just spectators, he thought, having too much fun—joking and teasing each other. If they were serious horseplayers, they'd pay closer attention.

"I like the gray," one said.

"Nope. His ass is too small," another answered. "Won't have enough speed in a short race."

Stupidity, Crawford thought. The conversation affirmed what he already felt sure of, that no one in this group knew anything about horses. Still, he admired the gray. Its color was beautiful: dark gray with a slight dapple. Normally, he wouldn't allow a horse's appearance to influence the way he bet, but this one was magnificent. He noted the horse's post position and decided to make a token wager.

He turned and found his path blocked by a man with a familiar face. At least he thought it was familiar. He was certain he had seen the man before, but he couldn't remember where.

"You're Hilton Crawford, aren't you?" The man spoke with a slight Cajun accent. It sounded more like the dialect of urban Cajuns, not the thick, homey sound of their swamp-living cousins.

Even though the voice was different, the disposition was similar to the Cajun people he knew from southern Louisiana. His smile was cordial, and Crawford grasped the offered hand without hesitation. "I'm sorry, I don't remember your name."

"It's Remington, R.L. Remington. And I don't think you'd have any reason to remember my name. We've never been intro-duced."

"Well, I know I've at least seen you around somewhere," said Crawford. He felt a little foolish. "I'm sure I know you from some-where."

"Oh yeah, we've seen each other around."

Remington seemed perfectly at ease. He was tall, taller even than Crawford. He dressed casually, but with obviously expensive taste. He was wearing a sports coat and jeans over alligator or lizard cowboy boots. His only jewelry was a gold Rolex with a diamond bezel. Yet, beneath the surface the man himself seemed of a lower caste, not some-one you would expect to see in expensive dressings. Maybe the image was what Crawford liked in him: a man who has achieved more than his social deserves.

"You've got a horse running in the eighth, don't you?" Already Remington seemed more friend than stranger.

"Yeah, Off to the Races," said Crawford. He assumed the next question before it was asked. "I'm not sure if he'll win, but he'll be a contender."

"You're pretty sure he'll be in the money then?"

"Yeah. My trainer thinks he's got a shot to win, but a show bet is pretty solid." Crawford was surprised at how easy this man was to know. "Stop by our table if you want. I'm here with my wife."

"No thanks," he replied. "I'm here with friends. Maybe I'll see you later, though." In fact, they did see each other again twice that night, before Crawford's horse ran and again afterward.

The seventh race was won by the horse with the too-small ass. Remington was greatly amused when Crawford shared the story of the conversation he had overheard. "What a stupid son-of-a-bitch," Remington replied. "Makes you wonder how he ever finds his way out of the parking lot."

In the eighth race they made matching wagers. Both men bet Off to the Races across the board, and both used him as the key horse in exacta combination bets. From number-four postposition he ran gamely, but was outdistanced in the stretch by a horse called Smokey Mountain. Still, by winning their place and show bets and a good exacta, they pocketed a nice profit.

Remington slapped Crawford's back. "Damn! You sure know your horses."

In truth, he knew very little, only what he had picked up in the last few months and what his trainer told him. Nonetheless, he enjoyed the praise. As the two men shook hands in parting, they exchanged numbers and Crawford extended an invitation for lunch if and when Remington should happen to be in the Houston area.

Crawford left the track a winner that night, but the weekend wasn't over. As often happens, Friday's win disappeared by the close of Sunday's races. It was the double-up and catch-up syndrome. For the true gambler, the one willing to put it all on the pass line for one roll, taking a small loss isn't an option worth considering. It might be the smart thing to do, but leaving loser while more races are on the card is like giving up the ballgame before time runs out. Walking away a loser is only for players without heart.

With four races left on Sunday, Crawford had been only a couple hundred down. But there's a trip-wire one crosses when it's close to leaving time. It's a little like putting a clock on a blackjack game—if you're a loser and know you can make only a limited number of bets, you start to double-up, to make bets you know are questionable. You lie to yourself, tell yourself a horse has a good chance of winning when you know it really doesn't. You fall into the make-believe world of gamblers, where good things happen when you need them to.

And sometimes they did. Sometimes Crawford would get down to his last hundred, his case money, and hit a winning combination that put him back in the plus column. He never lost hope, not as long as he had any money at all and there was another race to run. But this weekend, and many, many others, hope was not enough. He spent the three-hour drive back to Houston trying to figure out where the next bankroll was coming from.

VII

Even in the face of mounting financial pressures in 1991 nothing much changed, except that Crawford's characteristic optimism for a cause that many would have considered hopeless had been energized. Wasco's words about the looming sale of the struggling security company, although tentative, supported Crawford's self-image—he felt that once again he would pull a game out in the closing seconds.

The Christmas holidays came, and with them a family tradition originated by Crawford, the annual "money run." He filled his jacket pockets with currency, mostly ones but a few fives and tens as well—three or four hundred. His sons, Chris and Kevin, and sometimes a couple of their friends, would chase him. He ran, moving again like a high school athlete, swerving, fading, and dodging. Whenever he was touched, he threw a handful of bills into the air. The boys would scramble, bump and push, each trying to scoop up the most money. The excitement was contagious—even Connie sometimes joined in.

In prior years the game had included members of the University of Houston basketball team. Crawford sometimes invited foreign players, for whom going home was inconvenient, to join his family for holidays. Whoever was at their home during the game participated. One of the players was Rolando Farrari of Brazil, who later played for the Portland Trailblazers. Another was Rodger Fernandez, also of Brazil. Players of this caliber were a little quicker to the touch, but he could still make them run for the money.

Crawford listened eagerly when Charley Wasco told him a Chicago company, Corporate Investors, was interested in purchasing his company. He could hardly have heard better news. Perhaps he could rid himself of dealing with Sam Petro and come out with a little cash. He felt a rush, not the kind he got from the crap table or watching a horse race, more like the kind one feels from narrowly escaping the impact of an eighteen-wheeler.

There were still details to be worked out, but he was a motivated seller. He was ready to accept almost any offer, reasonable or not. Also, he knew Wasco and trusted him. Crawford knew there was no way Wasco would have approached him with an offer that wasn't solid—it was reason enough not to question the buyer's honesty.

Crawford met Robitusco, the potential buyer, at the airport. The Chicago man was a little overweight, with flashy jewelry and styled hair. He looked like a Vegas high-roller. He seemed somewhat out of place, maybe a little too smooth, but by now Crawford wanted out badly.

"Why are you interested in my company?" he asked.

"We're havin' growing pains," Robitusco said. He went on to explain that his company, based in Chicago, was interested in entering the Texas market. "We need your security license. Buyin' a company's quicker and easier than applying for a license. Everyone with our company is from Illinois, and Texas is pretty rough on out-of-state owners. With your license we'll be able to bid on federal contracts. Can't do it from outside the state."

It seemed reasonable. In fact, all his answers seemed reasonable— or maybe Crawford was overanxious and failed to see the warning signs. If he had stopped to think, he may have realized that the offer was too good to be true.

"It looks good. I like your operation," the Chicago man said. "Of course, we're goin' to need you to stay on. We need a man with your experience down here, so we can grow. You'll help us build." Not only did he offer an unrealistic sum for the struggling company—$280,000—but Crawford was to be retained with liberal salary and benefits. Crawford felt lucky, maybe a trip to Vegas would be in order when they closed the deal.

"We're goin' to arrange a wire transfer," the man told him. "It may take a few days. We've arranged a loan through one of our subsidiaries. It's a New York bank. We'll have to draw up the papers. The money will have to come from the bank to our subsidiary and then to us before we can wire it to you. There won't be any problems, though. You don't have to worry."

The Chicago firm was to pay $25,000 down and the rest in quarterly installments. Crawford agreed without reservation. Everything was on the up and up. There were contracts.

"Be sure to contact all your employees," he continued. "Salaries will remain the same for now, but the checks'll come from us. They can expect a healthy raise soon. You can tell'm that. And you'll need to contact your clients and let them know about the change. They'll need to start sendin' the payments to us." He made a clucking noise with his cheek. "We don't wanna get too top heavy with this payroll thing. We have to keep cash flow in balance—the first rule of business!"

Crawford nodded.

At first things seemed normal. Corporate Investors kept Crawford on as manager. They also gave Charley Wasco a supervisor's job as part of the agreement. Clients and employees adapted easily. There was no real change in their routine, just different signatures on the checks.

The first problem came three weeks after the changeover. Auditors found that paychecks were being issued to fictitious workers. The problem, they found, was that Colleen Hawthorne, the woman in charge of the office, had been embezzling. She had been fabricating personnel records and issuing checks to bogus employees, then depositing the funds into her own account. The amount stolen since the new company had taken over was around $5000.

The paper trail had been easy to follow—there was no question of Hawthorne's guilt. She was fired immediately, but she refused to repay any of the missing funds.

It was a dilemma for Crawford. She had likely stolen as much as sixty or seventy thousand over the months, and he wanted to go to the police. On the other hand, her father, Jim Gaffney, was manager of the Metro building, one of his biggest accounts, and if he filed charges he would probably lose Gaffney's business. To make matters even worse, if he lost that large an account, he worried that the sale might not go through.

Robitusco was angry. "Corporate Investors won't stand for this," he said. "I don't care if you file charges for the money she filched from you, but the $5000 she stole since my company took over is goin' to be reimbursed—or I'll file against her."

Crawford didn't think that he could get any of the money back by going to the police. He decided to forget about the money she had stolen before the changeover. For the $5000 Robitusco demanded, the two men went to her father.

Gaffney listened as they explained the problem.

"If I understand correctly," he replied. "You want me to pay for something my daughter did, or you're goin' to have her put in jail?"

Neither man answered.

"In the first place, it's my daughter you're talking about that did this, not me. I quit being responsible for her when she turned twenty-one. Besides, maybe it would be best for her to be charged. Might change her life for the better. But the fact of the matter is that I ain't about to be pickin' up her tab."

Robitusco seemed calm but determined. "So you'd see your own daughter sent to jail, rather than pay me the $5000 she embezzled? Even after Mr. Crawford has agreed to forget about the rest of the money?"

"Well, I guess if she goes to jail, I'll have to live with it. But what you two are doin' is called extortion, and I won't do business with you. Y'all gotta work this thing out between you, or I'll have to move my security contract."

Crawford began to see that the whole deal could fall apart over $5000. He turned to Robitusco. "Forget it. Just take the money out of my end."

Gaffney smiled. "Glad y'all can see my side of it."

VIII

The drive back from Shreveport to Conroe is long enough even after a winning weekend, but when you're busted, it seems like forever. A Johnny Mathis tape put rhythm to the monotonous sound of tires rolling away the uneasy images of loss. It takes some distance, some time, to shake off the feeling of losing—the bitter taste lingers like bile.

It might be different if he could be a little more like his friend, Billy Allen. Billy never seemed to take a loss hard. Oh sure, he'd get mad, might show some emotion, but he was always in control. He had seen Billy lose thousands of dollars on a fluke play in the closing seconds of a ballgame, then shrug and say, "Oh well, back to the drawing board." Crawford wanted to be more like that, it was just that he felt too deeply and held it inside. That complicated everything.

It didn't really have anything to do with greed, this involvement in gambling. Crawford was a generous man. He gave freely to almost anyone who asked. Can a person be generous and greedy at the same time? It was just that, to him, money had become—well, more than just money. It had become something like a way to score himself—to measure his ability, even his worth as a human being. It wasn't having or accumulating money. Crawford wasn't interested in being wealthy, but using money, spending it on his family and friends, as well as himself, then being savvy enough to go out and get some more. It was his fantasy, his opium. Nothing made him feel more alive!

His thoughts during the drive back were mostly on getting a new bankroll. You've got to have cash in order to gamble. He would check his credit cards, although he knew most of them were at their limit. He tried to remember. As he borrowed, and after a win, he usually paid some of the money toward his other cards in order to keep his credit limits as high as possible. It gave him leverage—leverage and flexibility. He understood the value of staying flexible. The availability of cash, even at high interest rates, was a necessity. Without funds he would be out of action. He wouldn't be able to earn what he needed to stay afloat, his nut. Everything would collapse. Everyone would see. Everybody would know how weak he was, that he was really no one special, just an ordinary man. All his imperfections, his faults, would be seen and pointed at, and people would turn away and forget him. He would disappear. Without the rush and the applause he would cease to exist.

Connie sat beside him in silence. He wondered what she would think if he was exposed as a failure. Would she still love him? He knew she would no longer trust or believe in him. The risk was too great. Losing Connie would be a greater loss than he could comprehend, greater even than the fear of death. No, he could never share with her the weight he felt. He would make everything okay, just as he had always done. She would never know.

As they crossed the Louisiana-Texas border Connie yawned. "It'll be good to be home." Crawford nodded and squeezed her hand.

IX

It was probably June, maybe even July, when Remington called. Whatever month it was, the call came early in the week and it was just after a successful road trip. Crawford felt like things were on the verge of turning for him.

"How you doing, Hilton?"

Crawford hesitated.

"I met you a couple of months ago. It's Remington, R. L. Remington."

Crawford remembered instantly the intense dark eyes, the Rolex, the confidence. Remington said he was going to be in Houston for a day or two and wondered if they could meet for lunch.

They met at The Pour House on 1960 just east of the interstate. At 2 o'clock the lunch crowd had already thinned. In the yuppie atmosphere, where slacks and tasseled loafers were the common dress, Remington's attire, lizard boots and jeans, seemed even more distinctive.

He looked different away from the track. Still confident and controlled, he acted like the two men had known each other forever. Away from the excitement of the crowded racetrack, though, Crawford saw Remington more clearly. His complexion seemed cloudy and dull, like a slight bruise. He had seen the look before, on the faces of his employees, the ones who worked only nights. And he had seen the look on men who had done prison time. He guessed that Remington was not a shift worker.

"Nice to see you, Hilton." The tone was sincere. It made Hilton feel good about coming.

"You too," said Crawford. He noticed the strength in the other man's handshake. "What brings you to Houston?"

Remington said that he was in town on business, but he was going to make time for the track. He wondered if Hilton wanted to come along.

Crawford declined. He liked the man and was pleased to get the invitation, but there was something unnerving about his presence. It was a little intimidating, made him feel uncomfortable. A short visit was just fine, but not an entire evening, not yet anyway.

They ate and chatted like old friends. They talked about horses, mainly about horses they had won money on, about football and basketball and about scams and schemes. Crawford told how he had acquired Off to the Races. About how the Allen brothers had held him back and then run him at an inflated price. About how they were then barred from Louisiana tracks and how they devised a complicated plot to transfer the horse's ownership to him. He enjoyed telling the story to people with similar interests, like a fisherman recalling a lunker bass story. The dark man listened intently.

Remington leaned in closer, the back of his hand touching Crawford's arm. "I wanna tell you something, Hilton." He lowered his voice. "If you ever need something done—anything at all—I can take care of it. I mean it. Anything."

Crawford didn't know how to answer. The implication sounded very sinister. But, who knew? There might come a time when knowing a man like Remington could come in handy. It was good that the man trusted him enough to offer, well, whatever he had offered. Besides, just being friends with him couldn't hurt anything.

"Thanks. I appreciate it," was the only answer that seemed appropriate.

Crawford came away feeling uneasy. Remington was nice, friendly enough. But it was like being in the company of someone untouchable, say a movie star; he enjoyed the man's company, but his presence was unnerving. And, as to the offer he had made, well, it made him glad they were friends rather than enemies.

X

After the Colleen Hawthorne incident things went smoothly for a while. Business seemed to go on as usual. The new company sent payment instructions to all the clients and began issuing payroll checks. Crawford was confident he had made the right decision.

But the first-quarterly installment did not come in as scheduled. Crawford treated the matter casually at first. Just technical stuff. He was sure the problems would soon work themselves out.

"Couple of minor problems with financing," the Chicago man told him. "We forgot to dot an *i* or put a dash where one's supposed to be. We had to resubmit the papers. Don't worry. We made sure everything was done right this time. Your money'll come in a few days."

It didn't come. There was always a new problem, one that Robitusco would explain, one that would be easily solved, according to the Chicago man. And then payroll checks began to bounce.

Robitusco became increasingly difficult to find. "Sorry, Mr. Crawford," the voice on the other end might say, "he's not expected in today. Try him again tomorrow. I know he's anxious to speak with you." Or, if Crawford seemed especially upset, "I'll try to contact him, Mr. Crawford." Sometimes they would actually talk, and there would be another excuse, but more often there was no word at all. After two or three weeks the calls became a daily routine.

Still, even after all the delays, Crawford was hopeful his money would come through. Corporate Investors paid for a trip to Chicago, where Robitusco again told stories of complex financial arrangements. "The money's on its way. We've had to move it through a couple of subsidiaries. This thing'll all be cleared up before you know it. Just bear with us a while longer." Even the first round of bad paychecks was explained away as a glitch.

Crawford was caught in the middle, trying to hold onto clients, while at the same time struggling to keep his employees from quitting. Many of the guards lived from one payday to the next. The urgency could be heard in their frantic phone calls. He did his best to soothe their anger and hold things together until the mess could work itself out.

Then came the second round of bad paychecks. Finally, when Crawford threatened to leave and take what was left of the business with him, the Chicago man agreed to a meeting. He still insisted that everything could be worked out.

Robitusco showed up at the Houston office with a personal bodyguard, something he hadn't done before. After listening for the better part of an hour to the same lies and empty promises he'd already heard, he finally realized that the Chicago deal had failed; maybe it had been nothing but an elaborate scam from the start. Crawford left, angrily announcing that he was taking his clients with him.

In all, three rounds of paychecks bounced before Crawford could regain control and have accounts transferred back into his name. Some clients had left already, citing the bad payroll checks as their reason. Crawford attempted to salvage what was left.

He felt responsible. It was his people who were hurt, the ones who admired and trusted him. Walking away wasn't an option. He talked to employees individually and promised them the checks would be covered—he would see to it. He didn't yet know how he would manage it, he only knew that he had to see things made right.

"I knew you'd help us," one of his men said. "I didn't know what was going on, but I never doubted that you would straighten this out. You're the only one we can count on." Crawford could no more have turned his back than if it had been one of his own children. Somehow, he had to find the money.

He was diligent and resourceful. Even though the dollar amount in hot checks swiftly climbed to almost $300,000, he swore to himself, as well as his employees, that he would make good the loss. First, though, he had to make sure the clients he had left would be with a solid firm. He had to make sure a fourth payroll didn't bounce.

He went to see his friend, Marvin Keller, who had been his supervisor in the old days. Keller had since left Pinkerton and begun his own firm. Ironically, he used the name of the old company for which they had both worked in the early '80s: Security Guard Service. Their friendship had lasted over the years. He was one of the few people to whom Crawford was close enough to confide.

Keller welcomed him. He knew Crawford well and trusted him, knew what a good employee he had been. The two men shook hands on a deal that would bring the remaining clients and employees into Security Guard Service. The agreement included a job for Crawford—

supervisor, just like the old days. But he still needed to honor the checks as he had promised.

After exhausting his savings, he borrowed on credit cards. It always surprised him how easy they were to get. In fact, he had begun to depend on them. It seemed that he got offers in the mail almost every day, and he frequently filled out applications and returned them. Some were in the name of Hilton Crawford, some H. L. Crawford, some another variation of his name. He lost track of how many cards he had—he usually just threw them in a drawer until he needed them. Whenever it became necessary, he used one card to pay off another. He had already taken a bankruptcy; he knew how easy it was to make debt disappear. With one New York bank he had five cards, each with a $7,500 limit—he maxed out all five. His savings and capital he borrowed totaled slightly less than $150,000. It wasn't enough.

In desperation, he committed his first serious crime, at least the first action that he himself thought was criminal. Defrauding credit card companies and casinos didn't fit the category. They weren't really criminal offenses in Crawford's view—it was just debt. It could be washed away with a bankruptcy. Lots of folks borrow more than they can repay. That's what the law's for, isn't it?

This time, however, he did something really illegal. He'd seen lots of people do it. Successful people, men he respected, had done it and gotten away with it. No one ever knew or cared. It was just an insurance scam, and everyone knew insurance companies had lots of money. If they didn't have enough, they just raised rates. The police didn't even seem to care. At least, when he was a policeman they didn't care much, not about covered losses.

He broke out the back window in his house and turned a couple of things over inside the house. Then he called police and reported a burglary. Officer Otis Johnson was sent to investigate. "Might a'come from them apartments behind y'all. There's a bad element lives in there," the policeman said.

"Yeah. I think maybe you're right. It doesn't matter, though. It's all insured. I just need a report."

Officer Johnson looked at the complainant curiously for several seconds. Crawford thought he probably knew, or at least suspected, but what could he do? There was no proof.

Connie's jewelry was reported stolen: all the rings, necklaces, earrings and baubles a wife collects over a thirty-year marriage. Almost all had been gifts from him, tokens of his love. The scam netted him another $50,000.

It still wasn't enough to satisfy the outstanding debt, but it was sufficient to demonstrate good faith to remaining employees and clients. The rest would have to wait.

Thoreau's famous quote, "The mass of men lead lives of quiet desperation," might have included Crawford but for the sentence that follows: "What is called resignation is confirmed desperation." Crawford acted desperately, but there was never even an illusion of resignation. Daily routine with family and friends never wavered. Even to the four or five close friends in whom he confided, his face never changed. He was always confident and optimistic. To be or think otherwise would have been to admit failure. Even his family never knew the extent of his financial problems.

When his son, Kevin, needed a couch for his college apartment, they looked for it together. The son picked a nice simple one for $800. "It won't do!" Crawford said. He felt the shame a parent feels whenever a child is deprived of something. "It isn't nice enough. You'll have friends visiting. You need something nicer for'm to sit on." They continued to shop until they found one that was appropriate, for almost twice the money. Crawford paid for it with a credit card.

Kevin probably wouldn't have been ashamed of the couch. It was, after all, just a couch—and he had picked it—but Crawford insisted. He had convinced himself that he would overcome the financial challenges he faced. His family would have whatever they needed.

XI

It was several weeks, maybe two or three months, before he heard from Remington again. He began to call occasionally, at irregular intervals. "Hello, how ya' doin'?" "Seein' any action?" Just friendly calls, like good salespeople make when they're following up leads.

One such call came after an especially bad weekend. Crawford's losing trips were becoming more frequent. The horses he owned won with reasonable constancy, but they couldn't make up for his losses. Cash to operate on, his bankroll, was increasingly harder to come by. Sometimes he won enough to get through the week, or the month, sometimes he didn't and had to resort to more creative means to pay what had to be paid, but he never gave up—he never reached what alcoholics and addicts call *the bottom*.

Remington was always courteous; he asked about Crawford's health and family before saying he was in Houston and was going to the track. "Jus wondered if m' old friend Hilton wanted to go along, maybe give me a lil' advice." His manner was easy, calling Crawford an old friend, and letting the words slide out softly.

Crawford told him of his bad timing. "Sorry, I can't make it this time." The weekend's loss was still fresh in his mind. "Just be glad you weren't with me this past weekend. If you had been listening to my advice, you mighta gone right down the toilet with me."

"Uh-oh. That don't sound good. Did'ya blow th' ranch?" It was more an expression of sympathy between gamblers than a direct question. *I understand the feeling. I've also lost heavily and I'm listening if you want to talk about it.*

"Fuck yes!" Crawford seldom used expletives to express himself. He thought it was common, degrading, and it made him uncomfortable. He liked to think he was above it, and insisted that his sons do likewise, but this was a private moment with a friend. The word seemed appropriate. "I never cashed a ticket. Didn't even stay for Sunday's races. Wasn't any point."

"Too bad. But shit, Hilton, didn't ya' mama tell you there'd be days like this?"

Crawford chuckled. "She never said there would be so many."

"Okay. So, when you gonna come and getcha money back?"

"I don't know. I've been doing pretty bad. Even having trouble coming up with entry fees."

Remington replied instantly. "Bullshit, Hilton. You know th' horses. You're a player. If ya' money's short, go out and get some more." Crawford had heard the expression before. It appealed to him.

"Uh-huh. That sounds good. Are you gonna to tell me how?"

There were several seconds of silence. He heard Remington breathe. When he heard the voice again it was quieter. "You know somebody that's got a lot of money? I don't mean somebody that jus lives in a big house and drives nice cars. All that don't really mean shit. I'm talkin' bout," his voice slower now, "somebody that's got a lot of cash. A big bookie maybe. Somebody that's really got money and can get their hands on it quick. You know somebody like that?"

The implication was menacing. *What is he talking about? Does he mean to rob somebody?* Crawford needed money, but he wasn't desperate enough to talk about something that sounded so ominous.

"No, not really. I can't think of anyone. I mean, well, I know people with money, but nobody that has a lot of cash."

There was an edge in Remington's response. "Well, you think about it, Hilton. You the one's got th' problem. I'm jus trying to help ya' with it."

When Crawford left the phone he felt an excited relief, like he had just gotten off an amusement ride. *How did Remington intend to get the money?* He had been afraid to ask, afraid to hear the answer for fear he might like it.

A lot of money? The thought was pervasive. Not only the words, but the way they were delivered. Remington seemed so confident. *He must know what he's doing. Whatever it is, he must have done it before. And didn't he say that we're friends?* Crawford didn't know how he would react if it came up again, but he was curious.

XII

Gambling—constant, up-close exposure to risk—becomes a need. At first it's only a temporary rush, but those who live with it know—they know they would be nothing without it, less than nothing, they would cease to exist. As a racehorse owner, Crawford's existence was never in doubt. The risk was constant, culminating only in an eventual race to the finish.

Joe Duhon was a good trainer. He was young, but he knew horses; he'd been around them all his life. When he offered advice, Crawford listened. "I'm tellin' you the horse can run," he said. "And this guy wants to sell. You need to go talk to him."

"I can't buy another racehorse. I don't have the money."

Duhon in his youth was emphatic. He was impatient. For him,

horses were more responsive than people, easier to work with. "I told you. Now it's been said. Do whatever you want."

"It's not that I don't believe you. I'd like to have another horse, especially one that can pay its own way. I just don't have the money. Do you think this guy might take some jewelry in trade?" Crawford still had Connie's jewelry, the jewelry he had reported stolen.

"I reckon he might. Won't hurt to talk to him."

The horse was Texas Roads. Its owner was a man called Buddy, who lived west of Houston, close to the small town of Sealy. The asking price was $5000.

"Jewelry? Sure. Come on out and we'll take a look at what you've got."

The man and his wife picked out a bracelet and ring set that had been made especially for Connie.

"How much you pay for it?"

"$9000. But that was a special price. I had it made for my wife." In truth, it had cost only $1500.

"Yeah. We like it. Trade even?"

"Well, I couldn't hardly do that. I'll trade for $1000 to boot."

Crawford felt a little guilty despite the fact that, as far as Connie knew, all her jewelry was lost. It had been gone for months. But he knew she missed it, and the set he was trading had been among her favorite pieces. Still, he was making a good trade. He had lied to the horse's owner about the value, but he felt no remorse for that. Horse-trading was an activity in which lying was acceptable, maybe even expected. And so Texas Roads became Crawford's second horse.

In the days to come Crawford's guilt plagued him ever more strongly, like shoes that don't quite fit. The prospect of owning Texas Roads had overshadowed the feeling at first, but Connie was still the most important thing in his life, even after more than three decades of marriage. She even mentioned it, how her hands looked so barren now. The tightness gathered and worked itself inward, forcing away the logic. He wanted her to be happy—he had promised her father.

As is often the case when one becomes dependent on deceit, lies become more outlandish, actions more brazen, more bizarre and desperate. Perhaps, for Crawford at least, there was also a sense of fulfillment in the act itself.

Crawford returned the rest of Connie's jewelry, but this time he needed a different lie. He didn't think he could again tell her it had been recovered in a pawnshop, as he did after his first insurance scam. Instead, he concocted a story about having the identical pieces made.

Connie must have suspected his lies. "This is strange, Hilton. There's a diamond missing from this ring, just like the other one."

"Huh? Let me see." He groped for an explanation.

"Sure is. Well, I gave him pictures and asked him to copy'm exactly. I didn't really mean for him to leave the diamond out though. Want me to take it back and have him put it in?"

"No, Hilton. Let's leave it like this. It'll remind me of what a thoughtful husband I have."

Part 6: Desperation

I

No one saw the gradual change in Crawford: the lies, manipulations, justifications. He allowed no one, especially those closest to him, to know what he felt inside. The feeling grew like kudzu. It took over, growing exponentially, until no one could tell the difference between the good man he once was and the bad man he was becoming, not even Crawford himself. It covered him, camouflaged and bound him. This insatiable vine grew from a fragment of thought, a single wretched seed that might be found in anyone who has the ability to think.

Friends and family saw only the Crawford they had always known. They saw a man who was energetic and fastidious, almost to the point of compulsion, who rose before the rest of his family to begin doing housework. In his closet were rows of unwrinkled slacks and shirts, all hung perfectly, separated by color and sorted from light to dark. They saw him feed and play with Roxie, the family's Rotwieller, who loved the pool and had her own float. They saw him answer the bell that he had given Kevin to ring from his upstairs room whenever he needed something. They saw the well-cared-for lawn. They did not see him complain or cry or even show the pain—things that most humans, the ones who can concede losses, do. They did not see or understand that Crawford had built a fragile world for himself and his family that existed within a sphere of his own making, and he could not allow anything to alter his creation. He would do whatever it took, and, in his mind, he *could* do whatever it took.

He didn't know he was changing, becoming something other than himself. He didn't realize he had begun to think like the people he used to arrest, like a villain. He didn't know it, but he must have felt it. In response, his body rebelled against him. His blood pressure soared to dangerous levels. He could feel the weakness growing inside him. He began to faint unexpectedly and had to be hospitalized. He was diagnosed as being at extreme risk of heart attack, and blood pressure medication was prescribed. Ironically, after his trial and death sentence, after all the lies had surfaced and all the sins were exposed, when the only remaining debt to pay was to surrender his life, his body returned to normal. He became again the Hilton Crawford of old.

II

Crawford's son Kevin was in college at the University of Houston and had his own apartment. But it was only fifty or so miles away, so he still came home most weekends. In fact, one could say he still lived in Conroe, just slept over by the University. He still had lots of friends in Conroe and still got his mail at home.

It was bringing in the mail that gave Crawford another idea for quick cash. He only intended to use it in case of emergency—in case he needed a temporary bankroll. He had helped his son, Kevin, apply for his first credit card, and after that the credit applications started coming in. It was crazy the way lending institutions went after him, a young man just starting his credit history. It seemed to Crawford that they should wait until someone has proven earning potential. They didn't seem to care, just kept trying to issue credit cards. "Take advantage of our introductory offer." "Special low interest rate for first-time users." "Special interest rates for students." So, indeed, Crawford took advantage. He began to fill out applications using his son's name. His cards were at their limit, and he could no longer get credit approved in his own name, although for a while he did use variations of his name—H. L. Crawford, H. Lewis Crawford—he rationalized that they were still him.

At first it was only five-hundred or a thousand at a time—just to keep up with entry fees at the track and a little to operate on. But the momentum of debt is insidious, and luck has a way of worsening when you need it most. By the time Crawford was arrested and the scheme was discovered, he had accumulated more than $70,000 of debt in his son's name.

No one knew. In likelihood, no one would have believed

anyway, not without the ability to see below the surface. They could only see the Bally shoes, the luxury vehicles, the signed pictures of celebrities crowding his walls. They didn't know what fragile images they saw, how nothing was as it seemed.

Crawford wondered what might happen. What if there came a time when he couldn't turn things around? He was in his fifties and they had no savings, no tangible assets except for the equity in his house. If that time ever came . . . ? But, to him, that *if* was the myth. His reality was in his own ability.

Once, while he was out of town, Connie agreed to purchase a lot in Pelican Bay, close to her sister's house. She was so excited when he came home he would never have considered saying no. Seeing her that way was worth whatever the cost. They went together to make the down payment. He had no idea how he would cover it, he just knew he would.

A similar incident occurred when Kevin needed $6000 for a headhunter fee. It was obvious he wanted the job badly. Crawford had only $1000 at the time. He went to Lake Charles that night, to the riverboat casinos, and played blackjack. He left when he was $6500 ahead and paid the agency's fee the following day.

Nobody, not even Crawford himself, recognized the desperate fragility of his world. Perhaps if he could have separated himself from the responsibility he willed upon himself, could have simply paused for a time, maybe then he could have seen that something would happen—that he was going to do something he would regret.

(From death row, eleven months before his execution, Crawford wrote: "I just wish now I would have talked to her, but my pride got me, and my pride got me in here. I hope and pray the book will show the love I had for my family. I gave them everything I could while they asked for nothing. They were my joy, and I hurt them. My life is very lonely now, with a piece of my heart missing. All this was a tragedy for the Everetts and a tragedy for my family and friends.")

III

Marvin Keller was a good friend and a knowing boss. He understood Crawford's strengths and weaknesses as well as anyone, and he knew how important it was for Crawford to reduce his debt. He wanted to help. Keller was planning a start-up shipping business and told Crawford that if it was successful, he would help pay off what he owed. Crawford was easily optimistic. He knew nothing about the shipping business, but he knew Marvin Keller—if anyone could make it work, it would be him.

Keller brought in a man called Jon Olsen from Panama, who was said to be an expert. Olsen lined up cargo from one port of call to another, with the success of each leg of the journey depending on the previous trip for expenses. For the maiden voyage, Crawford stayed on the sidelines—he had no money to contribute. Maybe next time out he would be in a better position. He might have money then. Surely his unlucky streak wouldn't go on for much longer.

Keller and Olsen's first venture was with a Greek ship called *Sea Lady*. It was to pick up cargo in Baltimore, then sail to Chile, where it would pick up a load of fishmeal bound for China. *Sea Lady* was never able to collect her first load. A collision blocked the Baltimore channel to incoming vessels for several days. The shipping contract was lost because of the late arrival, and *Sea Lady* steamed back to Greece without cargo. Keller and his backers lost all their original investment, around $150,000.

IV

The second shipping venture, the one in which Crawford had a financial stake, came after he and Allen had pulled off another successful racing scam. Crawford was becoming bolder, more desperate in his actions. The money he was making in salary wasn't enough. He was barely managing to stay current on everything by paying the interest.

His plan was simple and bold, and centered around Rather Rapid, the third horse Crawford acquired. Rather Rapid could run. Joe Duhon knew the horse and its history. He knew the horse was an underrated claimer. But the best thing about this horse was its appearance—it looked exactly like a washed-up horse called Come Along Kid. The two horses were identical, except for the way racehorses are marked: a tattooed number inside the lower lip.

Allen wasn't sure about it. The scam had been used as long as there had been horse races—just switch horses and run a winner in place of a loser. It was risky. "So you really think it'll work?"

"Yeah. You've seen this guy. He's scared of the horses. He won't check a skittish horse." Allen convinced Crawford it was worth the risk. When Come Along Kid was scheduled to run, they would replace him with Rather Rapid.

The timing had to be perfect. Both men were in the paddock helping ready the horse. Allen stood at the horse's head; it was supposedly his horse. Crawford was on the other side, at the horse's flank. The official came, clipboard under his arm, and spoke to Allen. As he reached for the halter to pull the horses head toward him so that he could check the tattoo, Crawford used his elbow. He jammed it into the sensitive part of the horse's flank. Rather Rapid responded just as they had expected. He jerked his head backward and reared slightly, as if he was responding to the official's reach.

"Whoa, easy boy." The official reached again, and again Crawford spooked the horse. This time the official dropped his clipboard.

"He's a little anxious today, huh?" He picked up his board and brushed away the straw and muck. He didn't speak again, just made a mark on the paper and went on to the next horse.

Rather Rapid won easily. Seven years later Crawford couldn't remember exactly how much was wagered or what kinds of bets were made, but he did remember that a $2 win ticket paid $34.60. A gambler's memory is peculiar that way. It's easy to remember details of a win, but losses are more difficult. He recalled that his end of the total collected was around $12,000.

V

Olson, the man Keller hired to run the shipping business, was confident there would be no further problems. He and Keller planned to hire another ship, a smaller ship this time so the risk wouldn't be as great. They needed start-up money, but most of the original investors had been scared away by *Sea Lady's* failure. The biggest losers didn't want to chance the same thing happening again. Olson explained that it was just a fluke, a freak occurrence, but they weren't convinced.

Crawford, however, was ready to take the gamble. This time

he had cash to invest from the Rather Rapid switch. He had around $10,000 remaining, not enough to make much of a difference in what he owed. He needed to parlay the money, to invest in something that could result in enormous returns. Olson's description of compounded profits made the investment sound like the perfect opportunity. Crawford thought it might be his only chance. It was late in the ballgame, and he needed a grand slam, but he'd done it before, he knew he could do it again.

He gave Keller the $10,000, but Keller and Olson had not yet been able to raise the balance of the money they needed for the second venture. Crawford wanted it to work. He had convinced himself that the shipping deal was going to return windfall profits and become the way out of his financial mess. It was to this end that Crawford made a call he later regretted—he called Pat Foster, his old friend. Foster had left the University of Houston and was coaching in Reno. Crawford told him about the profit potential. His enthusiasm must have been contagious, because Foster became equally convinced. He sent Crawford $40,000 to invest for him.

Money, however unfortunately, has a way of testing friendship. When weeks passed without word of his investment, Foster began to call. He was worried, and his friend couldn't provide the answers he wanted. Crawford trusted Keller and had simply assumed that he had checked the venture out thoroughly. He told Foster, "If Keller trusts Olson and has confidence in him, it's good enough for me." His friend, Keller, would let him know whenever there was any news, good or bad. Until then Crawford had no interest in knowing details about cargo and ships.

For Foster, however, assumptions of trust weren't enough. He wanted to know how his money was being spent, and when his friend could not provide that information, Foster grew impatient. He cursed Crawford for getting him involved in something he didn't know more about and demanded his money back. Crawford was told it was too late. The money had been obligated and could not be returned. The long-time friendship between Foster and Crawford was over.

The loss of his friend hurt more than any loss he had ever taken. Crawford cried after Foster's call, and swore that he would get the money back for him. He didn't know how but he would get it back. He promised himself that he would somehow get the money and pay Foster out of his own pocket. He considered it a debt of honor.

VI

As his debt spread out of control like an untended brush fire, Crawford spent his days with no outward display of emotion, save those of design meant for others. He was compartmentalized, separated into what he thought he should be for everyone else—and his concept of what everyone else thought he should be for himself. And, maybe that's who he really was, everything to everyone—good, bad, caring, narcissistic, he seemed to fit all the roles. He wore one face for his family, another for his employees, still others for friends and gambling associates. He was simultaneously weak and strong. His straw world became more fragile with each passing day, and he lived with the fear that something would happen. It could be anything, perhaps it would be something insignificant, something he had never thought of, that could happen and cause his world to collapse. Then everyone would know, would know who he really was. Or even worse—he would know himself.

It was during this time of desperation that Remington made one of his periodic calls. Now Crawford was past the point of being receptive; one could say he was even anxious. He had thought more about their earlier conversation. *A lot of money*—that's what Remington had said.

"You remember offering to help me make some money?"

"Yeah, Hilton. And I meant it."

"Well, supposing, just *supposing*, I did know someone who had a lot of cash, then what?"

Remington didn't answer right away. "Hilton, we're friends, right?"

"Sure. Yeah."

Remington continued to pause between replies, letting the words drift out slowly, like a gathering fog. "Well, you know I think a lot of you. If I didn't like you, I wouldn't be telling you this."

"Arright." Crawford waited.

"Understand—I'm doin' this to help *you*." Another pause. "Here's how it works. You find someone's got a lot of cash. And they gotta have kids, gotta have a kid they really care about."

Crawford stopped him. "You talking about kidnapping some-body?"

"Don't get ahead of me, Hilton." He sounded impatient. "It sounds like kidnapping, but it ain't—not exactly. Besides, I've done this before—I know what I'm doing."

"Yeah, okay. Go ahead."

"You take the kid and baby-sit it a while, then you let it go. Meanwhile, you call the parents and tell'm if they wanna see the little darlin' again, they need to up the cash. Most of the time they pay right away. If they don't pay—fuck it—just forget it. You don't screw around negotiating and all that shit—that's when you get in trouble. Either way, pay or not, you turn the kid loose after a couple'a days. Hell, sometimes they're already on the way home while we're out pickin' up the money. If, maybe say the old man's a hard-ass and doesn't want to pay, the only thing we're out is a little time. When the kid shows back up in a couple of days everybody's happy—shit, they think it's Christmas. And the police, hell, they're not gonna waste a lotta time tryin to solve a case where nobody gets hurt."

"I don't know . . . *kidnapping?*"

"Trust me, Hilton. It'll work. I've done this before. Nobody gets hurt. It's easy as shootin' ducks on the water."

"I'll think about it." He was ready to end the conversation.

He suspected Remington of exaggerating. *Can it really be that easy? He said he's done it before. And there's all the debt—and Kevin's credit cards.*

VII

When a seed is ready to germinate, the delicate protective coating melts, breaking away, allowing the embryo to sprout. Remington had sown the seed, and feeding it were memories left by Everett. Crawford saw the continuing sales push to join Amway as manipulative and self-serving. *He says he's got money—$500,000 in one account, $750,000 in another. He got it easy. Down-line made it for him. If he got it easy, he'll give it up easy. Give it up for something he cares about, anyway.*

Crawford's thoughts fed on themselves, the way anger builds until something finally happens. Only it wasn't exactly anger he felt, it was something else, something like judging someone, then justifying that judgment as resentment or hatred. It's almost instinctual. If one wants to dislike someone, it is usually easy to find a reason.

He remembered an oil deal from back in the 1980s. It had been a friendship thing. Everett was a land-man in the oil and gas industry and often put deals together. He told Crawford and another friend, Fred Pierce, about a promising lease near Baytown. He needed investors. Crawford recalled putting in around $10,000 and Pierce the same, but there was no paperwork. Months passed and little was mentioned about the well until the two men finally called Everett and asked him directly. "Sorry, I've been meaning to call you guys. The hole was dry."

The resentment Crawford had felt back then came bubbling back. *Just like that, he told us. Never even gave us any paperwork for the IRS. And when I asked him to show me the well, he kept making excuses why he couldn't do it. Yeah, I'm pretty sure he snapped us off. He ought to have something coming to him for that—for screwing his friends.*

The ugliness inside Crawford spread. He began talking with Remington about kidnapping McKay. He would later describe the feeling as they planned it, even as they actually took him, as unreal, more like a dream than real life. "I just kind of thought we had just been talking, that it wouldn't really happen, that any moment we would stop and not really do it."

They decided the Amway meeting would be a good time. The Everetts usually left McKay at home by himself, and they'd be gone for a predictable time—time enough to get the job done.

"You need somebody to make the ransom call," Remington said. "Better make it a woman, confuse'm a little. I can take care of it if you don't know anybody."

"No. I know a woman that I think will do it. She'll be good."

He mentioned Irene Flores, the feisty little lesbian who had worked for him before she was arrested and did time for drug possession. After being discharged from prison, she could no longer work in the security industry, but she and Crawford remained friends. Crawford liked hiring lesbians. He thought they were more responsible and harder workers. And Irene was well liked, popular with the gay crowd. She sent him lots of applicants.

"And we're going to need a baby-sitter. Somebody to keep the kid outta sight for a few days. It's gotta be somebody clean and somebody we can trust. I know a couple of people if you don't."

It was decided. Remington would make the grab. They would do it without letting McKay see Crawford. They would put a hood over the boy's face and drive him to Louisiana, where they would meet a friend of Remington's. The third man, whom Crawford had not met, would take McKay to New Orleans for a few days then turn him loose at the bus station with enough money to make the trip back to Conroe.

"Sounds okay. Sounds good," Crawford said. It was what he said whenever he wanted something to happen, or if he wanted to appease someone. "Okay, sounds good." He had said it to the men who convinced him to run for sheriff of Jefferson County. He had said it to Connie when she wanted a bigger house. He had said it to Sam Robotusco. And said it to Sam Petro. And said it to Charles Kalil. And he would later say it to the defense lawyers whose job it was to keep him from the execution chamber.

But for now, he said it to Remington. "Okay. Sounds good."

I trust that these things will happen as you say they will happen.

Part 7: The Kidnapping

I

Tuesday, September 12, the day of the kidnapping, passed for Crawford like many of his recent days. It was a dark time. He felt like he was a fictional character acting out a role in a play or movie, or maybe a dream. Uneasy REM sleep, where there's a sudden change, from confidence to doubt. Going the wrong way. Needing to stop and can't. *Don't stop. Never stop. Never quit.*

It probably won't happen, Crawford thought. *Probably be like last time, when Paulette decided not to go to the meeting. Something will happen. Something will stop us. Remington won't show up. He wasn't serious about doing this. It was all just talk. We won't go through with this. We can't. Something will stop us.*

Crawford didn't see Remington when he first pulled into the Randall's center at I-45 and the loop. They were supposed to meet at the corner, by Clayton's Jewelry, but Remington wasn't there. It seemed to be just like he thought it would be, just a game, just talk. Then he saw. The other man had seen him first, and was walking toward him from the direction of the supermarket. He stopped the car and waited.

Remington threw a gym bag into the back seat. "You ready?" He seemed almost enthusiastic, like they were about to enjoy a night of league bowling.

"I didn't see you. You were supposed to be on the corner."

"Think about it, man. Standing in front of a jewelry store with a gym bag—how fuckin' smart is that? You never told me about the Goddamn jewelry store."

"Okay. Yeah, I see. I'm not too used to this. I'm sorry."

"It's okay. No harm done. We just need to pay attention to

details. It's not thinking about things like that that might fuck this up. We need to think everything out. You damn sure the kid'll be by himself tonight?

"Nobody'll be home. I called twice just to make sure. They're expecting me at the Amway meeting. I'm supposed to bring a couple of prospects. I told you this guy is gung-ho. He would never miss a chance to sign up somebody new."

Remington took a blue shirt and badge from the bag as they drove toward the Everett home. It was only a ten-minute drive to the upper-middle-class Conroe neighborhood. He was methodical and seldom smiled. After all the buttons were fastened, he asked for Crawford's approval.

"You'll do, I guess." Crawford hesitated. "Are you sure this will work? I mean, you have done this before?"

Remington looked at him.

"I just want to be sure, that's all."

"Like I told you, everything'll be fine. Just trust me."

II

It was sometime after 8 p.m. when they turned onto the Everetts' street. Crawford had described the house in detail, but it was the first time Remington had seen it.

"Pull past the house and turn around. If there's a problem, if somebody else is in there, I don't want them to see the car." There was nothing tentative in Remington's voice. He was under control and in control, like he was accustomed to tense situations. Crawford was just the opposite. He felt the rush holding him, pushing him forward, not letting him think about what he was doing.

"I'll motion to you when I'm ready for you to pull into the driveway. And when I do, I don't want any fuckin' around. I want you in there fast. Get as close as you can to the door, right in front of it, and pop the trunk. You ready?"

Crawford nodded. He watched as Remington walked across the yard. His view was obstructed. He pulled forward a little so he could see. He watched Remington ring the bell. Then the gesticulations. In the blue uniform Crawford thought it looked as if he was directing traffic. The door opened and he made a quick motion. Almost instantly he was inside. That's when Crawford finally understood that it was really happening. They were kidnapping McKay.

Crawford did as instructed. He parked in front of the door and pushed the trunk lever. *Too late now. Too late to stop.* He continued through the motions. It had been agreed.

Crawford saw Remington come out carrying a hooded and struggling McKay. He heard and felt McKay's body as it was thrown into the trunk. The lid was slammed, and suddenly Remington was sitting in the passenger seat again.

It's real—It's done.

"Let's go, man. Get us out of here."

There was no verbal response. Crawford sent the car backward out of the driveway. Momentum carried the LHS across the street, almost bumping a garbage can.

"I think I hit—"

"Fuck it! Drive!"

The Chrysler lunged forward. Neither man had noticed the figure standing beside the garbage cans.

The vehicle wasn't made for tight cornering. Tires screeched, stabbing through the serene darkness of McKay's neighborhood. Remington sharply punched the side of Crawford's leg. "Easy man—slow down."

He didn't slow down. He heard the voice but didn't assimilate the thought. His body was experiencing a sort of constant, spontaneous quiver. He was in the dream-state, fixed and functioning but without judgment. He wasn't exactly forgetting, it was more closely akin to overlooking things. Then he ran a stop sign.

"Pull over," Remington said. It was a command. Crawford slowed to a stop at curbside.

The sound was more startling than the pain as Remington slapped Crawford's chest. He grabbed a handful of shirt and pulled the older man closer to him so that they faced each other. "You dumb motherfucker. You stupid son-of-a-bitch." The words came in furious succession. "You don't speed! You don't run stop signs! You don't do anything that might get us noticed." He paused for breath. "Have you forgotten we've got a kid in the fucking trunk?"

Crawford mumbled an apology.

"Don't be sorry, Goddammit. Just get us to Louisiana."

Crawford contained his anxiety long enough to get to the loop and move in an easterly direction. He was functioning, moving the way they had planned. However, a sickening realization struck him as they approached the interstate. He wanted to remain silent, just drive and let whatever was to happen happen. Yet he knew he couldn't. It was a careless error on his part, and it had to be addressed. He cleared his throat. "We're going to need to stop for gas."

"What? You didn't fill up before you picked me up?"

"No, damn it, I didn't." His voice was breaking. "I—I just didn't think about it."

Remington could see that he was on the verge of losing control. "Okay, just calm down. Look for a place where there's no one else at the pumps."

Crawford tried to think of which station might have the fewest customers. While he explored the possibilities, another thought came to him. He had almost no money. He decided against checking his wallet with Remington in the car. He remembered having only three or four dollars, not enough to buy gas. *How could someone who is going to kidnap a child not think of bringing money? What if something goes wrong? Gas can be bought with a credit card, but what if something else happens, some emergency? And credit cards can be traced. Stupid . . . Stupid.*

He found a Diamond Shamrock store with no one around. As he pumped the gasoline, he listened for noise coming from inside the trunk. There was no sound. He thought briefly about opening the lid just enough to check on McKay, but reconsidered. *Don't want to mess things up any more than they already are.* He finished pumping, went inside, and used a credit card to pay for his gas. Remington had not spoken and remained silent when he came back to the car.

He didn't speak again until they reached the outskirts of Conroe. "It's time you made the call," he said. "Try not to fuck *this* up!"

Crawford called Irene Flores from his cellular phone. The message was simple. They had already discussed what she would say. He had given her the telephone number and Carl's first name. "We've got him," he said.

Flores responded by saying that she was going to a pay phone. "I'll keep on calling until I get an answer."

Neither man spoke after the call. No acknowledgement was needed or wanted. Crawford drove on in his dream-state, while Remington seemed to have retreated to his own world of thought.

III

The first leg of the journey was to Cleveland by way of Highway 105, through the town of Cut and Shoot and then a twenty-mile stretch of road lined with flea markets, dilapidated mobile homes, and wrecking yards. Along the way are several burned-out buildings. Crawford had, on an earlier trip along this road, remarked that it seemed a likely area for spontaneous combustion. This time, however, he didn't think or even notice the area. Passing the burned shells of failed businesses just seemed like window dressing for an already somber mood.

They followed 105 all the way to Beaumont. After Cleveland, the scenery changed a little, but not the mood. Tension between the two men was thick in the air, like the smell of road kill. At Beaumont they turned onto I-10 east toward Lafayette.

Thirty minutes into Louisiana they began to hear noises from the trunk. Bumps and cries. Muffled sounds, unintelligible but easily interpreted as McKay's fear and desperation. Crawford wondered if they should stop and check on him.

"No. He can't hurt nothing back there," Remington responded. "Call Flores back and make sure she got hold of his old man."

Crawford used his cellular phone to call Flores. Her mother told Crawford in broken English that Irene had gone out and had not said when she would return.

"She hasn't gone home yet," Crawford told Remington.

"Goddamnit."

"I told her to go straight home. I told her to make the call and go home." It was a lie. Crawford didn't remember exactly what he had told her, but he couldn't admit that to Remington. "Maybe something happened. Maybe she couldn't get them right away. Maybe they went somewhere after the meeting." He knew that wasn't the case. They would never leave McKay alone so late.

"Fuck that! Maybe the stupid bitch never even *made* the call!"

"That's not like Irene. She wouldn't just leave us hanging. I know she made the call."

"You know? You *know*? You don't even know enough to fill up the car with gas!" Remington was angry, so much so that Crawford didn't try to respond. "Fuck it! We'll try again later."

Crawford drove on in silence. It was late enough that traffic was light and headlights skimmed the treeline. Live Oaks, huge and misshapen with age, dominant in blacks and grays. They slid by, gnarled fingers pointing, frowning behind their mossy beards. They seemed an appropriate background for the dream as it floated him forward, farther along the course plotted for him over a lifetime.

Only the occasional sounds of McKay's struggling interfered with road rhythm. When Remington finally spoke again, it was with an urgency that seemed to overshadow his anger.

"Call the bitch again." This time they were within thirty minutes of Lafayette.

"Goddamn bitch has gotta be there by now," he mumbled as Crawford dialed. "How'd I know this deal was gonna be fucked?"

Again Flores' mother answered the phone.

"Not yet? She hasn't come home yet?"

"Fucking idiots. Motherfucking amateurs." Remington's angry interjections made it difficult for Crawford to hear. The mother's difficulty with English further complicated things.

"When she comes home," Crawford spoke slowly and loudly so he could be heard over his partner's ranting, "ask her to stay there."

"This deal is fucked, Goddamnit! Goddamn fucking morons! Been fucked from the start!"

"Please ask her not to leave. It's very important that I speak with her."

She agreed. Of course she would tell Irene to stay. In the background she could hear an outraged voice. She couldn't make out the words, only that the other man was angry and cursing. (Her acknowledgement of the second voice was never mentioned during the trial. Afterward, she wrote to Irene and told her that her friend must have been telling the truth about another man because she had heard his voice. She said she never told authorities because no one ever asked.)

Crawford estimated that they had come to within twenty to

thirty miles of Lafayette. There had been occasional noises coming from the trunk, but now they intensified. They sounded louder, more desperate. Perhaps McKay had become more nervous in response to Remington's angry ranting. Then there was silence—only road noise—no sound from the trunk. Even Remington seemed in momentary repose, heavy with thought.

The quiet was broken by the clunk and scrape of metal on metal. Both men realized its meaning. It was the sound of a pry-bar being used inside the trunk. McKay was trying to lever open the trunk lid. Remington glared at Crawford. "Shit! You left a fuckin' lug wrench back there, didn't you?" Without waiting for an answer he ordered, "Pull this motherfucker over!"

"Here?"

"Right here! Right now!"

Crawford obeyed. He slowed and moved the Chrysler to the highway shoulder. "Open the fuckin' trunk," Remington commanded as he jumped from the vehicle even as its wheels continued to roll.

Crawford sat still, indecisive, yet somehow aware that the uneasy dream world sequence in which his day had passed was becoming, or had already become, a reality of nightmarish extent. He sat and listened to sounds that could only mean McKay was being beaten. Dullish thuds, not more than two or three. Then it was over and Remington was back in his seat.

"What happened," Crawford asked, in spite of the fact that he already knew. "What did you do? Nobody was supposed to get hurt!"

"Get goin'. He'll be all right, he just won't make any more noise for a while." After hesitating, Remington added, "I think he may have cut his arm on something, though."

"How bad is he hurt?" Crawford asked as he pulled back onto the highway.

"I told you, he'll be fine." He shrugged and added, "Hell, why worry about it now. What's done is done."

Crawford had no answer. If he had thought about it, really planned everything, he wouldn't have left the lug wrench in there. He just didn't think. He didn't think it was really going to happen. It had unfolded like a dream—that he stepped into and just kept walking through—that just wouldn't end. It was like a bad run at the tables, when you can feel the bad things about to happen and you don't stop—you keep stacking your money on the pass line and, even before you do it, you know you're going to lose. And you know you won't stop until you lose it all—until everything is gone—everything.

They drove in silence for the next several miles, maybe ten, before Remington said to exit and pull up behind a waiting burgundy Cadillac. This would be the contact man, where they were to make the switch. The other man was to take McKay on to New Orleans. After two or three days he would be put on a bus back to Texas, and it would all be over. That was the way it was supposed to happen. That was what Crawford expected to happen—it was what he wanted to happen. But the gambler's warning had sounded. *You might sweat, maybe get a little nauseous, but you don't stop.*

The other man was alone. Crawford could see that he was heavy-set and perhaps dark-skinned. That must have been how Remington got to Conroe. Maybe his partner dropped him off and came back to Louisiana. Or maybe he stuck around and followed. Maybe he was watching to see that everything went okay and then went ahead to wait. Remington sat on the passenger side. Crawford watched what seemed to be an animated conversation. Remington's hands would suddenly fly to seat level. His head would turn violently from side to side. It was easy to see he was angry—but Crawford already knew that.

The men concluded their conversation in less than five or six minutes, although it seemed longer. Remington returned to the Chrysler. "Follow him," he said. "Be damn sure you don't lose him."

"What's going on?"

"I'll tell you what's going on." His voice now seemed more resolute than angry. "This deal is over. It's fucked. That's what's going on. You and your little dyke buddy have screwed this thing up from the start. We had a chance to make some money here, but no more—the chance is gone." He inhaled deeply, hesitating a few moments. "Aw hell, Hilton. You know I like you. I just gave you too much credit. I shoulda known you couldn't pull this off."

Crawford drove in stunned silence. He still didn't fully comprehend. All he understood was that the kidnapping plan had failed and Remington had said it was over. He didn't know if he would be left alive, if McKay would be left alive with him. But whatever the eventuality, he knew it was over, and that brought a strange sense of relief. He had willingly stepped over a line that could not be recrossed, but he would not go further. He saw the Cadillac exit under a sign marked *Whiskey Bay*.

"Stay behind him."

Crawford obeyed mechanically. They followed the other car onto a poorly maintained access road that circled back, leading down to the level of the swamp, then turned north underneath the freeway. The headlights moved ahead through the road's curve, revealing a thick roadside growth of yellowing weeds. Through the shadows were white glimpses of discarded appliances and bulky outlines of worn-out automobile tires. The area was remote enough to be used by passers-by as a dumping ground for possessions that could no longer fill their purpose.

The road surface changed abruptly from crumbling asphalt to shell. But even the paved portions had contained potholes filled with opaque swamp water, making their depth uncertain. Crawford watched the Cadillac splash forward and pull into what appeared to be a driveway. "Pull over behind him," said Remington.

Crawford drove just past and parked so that the trunks of both vehicles were only yards apart. He wanted to believe that McKay would be all right, that he would be transferred to the stranger's trunk and taken on to New Orleans. He wanted to believe that all Remington had meant when he said the "deal is over" was that there would be no further ransom demand. That was his understanding—*if anything goes wrong he goes on a bus and is sent back to Texas.* He wanted to believe these things, but again came his gambler's instinct. *Things will not get better, only worse.* He fought against the feeling, tried to dispel the negative energy.

The Cadillac's headlights showed a galvanized aluminum gate, the type used in farm country. Beyond the gate was the outline of what appeared to be a house, old and weathered, but with a shiny tin roof. Then darkness, as the other man turned off his lights. *Surely they wouldn't pull into the driveway of someone's home to make the switch.*

"Whose house is this?" he asked.

Remington didn't answer. He said simply, "Open the trunk." As he stepped out, he opened his stance widely to avoid a puddle.

The Cadillac's driver seemed amused. "Worried about your boots?" he asked, grinning. "That skin always worked good when it was on the fuckin' lizard."

Crawford pressed the trunk release and stepped onto the shell road. Swamp smell was strong—the odor of rotting vegetation. He walked to the rear of the car and looked in at McKay. The boy lay still, perhaps already lifeless. His hair and clothing were saturated with blood, his features distorted. Reality broke through the forced optimism. He gripped the edge of the trunk for support.

Remington wasted no time—he picked up the child's legs while the other man grabbed one arm. Together they hoisted McKay's body from the vehicle, carried him to the edge of the shallow bar ditch, and laid him among the jimson weed and sunflowers.

Crawford stood without comprehension even as the Cadillac driver moved away from McKay. Remington stepped back to the car and leaned into the trunk. He picked up Crawford's gun case.

"Somethin' else you musta forgot."

It was true. Crawford didn't remember it was in the trunk. It had been among the gym bags and papers, close to where McKay's feet had been. Remington unzipped the case.

"I guess we're lucky the kid didn't find *this* when he was lookin' for somethin' to pry with."

Sound triggered Crawford's awareness—the sound of Remington racking the .45, sending a cartridge into the chamber. The impersonal metallic noise instantly confirmed what Crawford had not allowed himself to admit.

"No, you—" He lunged forward as Remington fired the first shot and felt blood spatters as the shock wave hit his body. It felt like someone had thrown a handful of rice. He was closer as the pistol exploded a second time. He twisted spontaneously, shielding his face and felt the spray burst against his back. He had waited too long and done too little. McKay was gone.

He stood in stunned silence as the two men carried McKay's body to the gate and hoisted it to the other side. It was done efficiently. They might have been dockworkers, moving a final sack of grain before the end of their shift. He listened to the crunch of weeds and brush as they drug the body away from the roadway. He heard their muffled voices as they returned.

Remington wiped his prints from the gun. He dropped the .45 into the trunk and closed the lid. "We coulda made some money," he said. "But what the hell. Sometimes you gotta cut your losses."

Crawford didn't answer.

"You know we had to do this, right? It's too bad about the kid, but we didn't have no choice. It had to be done. You see that, don't you?"

Crawford nodded. "I guess."

"You know Goddamn well it did! This thing was all fucked up. We coulda been in a shitstorm if we'd tried to keep him alive."

Crawford nodded again.

"Shit, Hilton. Just get in that car and get your ass on back to Texas and remember to keep your fucking mouth shut and everything will be all right. Just be cool and take care of business and nobody else will have to get hurt."

Crawford found the driver's seat and started the engine. The Cadillac was in the driveway and the road was too narrow for a u-turn so, unthinking, he pulled forward, farther into the swamp. *Sooner or later there'll be a place to turn around.* In his rear-view mirror he saw the Cadillac's taillights as it moved toward the interstate.

IV

It was over—McKay was dead. Fear and guilt consumed Crawford to the point that his logical thought processes were skewed. He wasn't a professional criminal, but he had tracked down and arrested many who were. His experience as a law officer was extensive enough to teach him how to make his tracks more difficult to follow. But he didn't. He made only the careless attempts of an amateur. His actions were quickly conceived and born of desperate fear. Yet the fear was not for his life, rather for his *way of life*. He feared the contempt of his family and friends. Moreover, he feared facing his mirrored image—the pain of self-acknowledgement, realizing who and what he had become.

During the coming week Crawford would be plagued with guilt for the horror he had caused, until he confessed and told officials where to find the body. After, he could close his eyes. After, he didn't have to see or hear. It was finally out of his hands.

The same was not true, however, for the other citizens of Conroe and the surrounding area. Monday newspapers carried the whole story. People were enraged. The brutality of the crime committed by one of their own—they felt betrayed. Not only had a beautiful child been murdered, taken from behind locked door and alarm, taken by a trusted friend who could have been neighbor to any of them, taken and beaten and killed and left in the muck of a Louisiana swamp. Not only had the Everetts been robbed of a son and McKay robbed of life—they, all of them, had been robbed of the notion of trust. They were no longer who they thought they were. Hilton Crawford had taken it all away. Overnight he became, in the words of his own attorney, *the most hated man in all of Montgomery County.*

Counselors were called into area schools. Ministers led their congregations in prayers for healing. Around the state, newspaper headlines referred to Crawford as *Uncle Hilty.* The story stayed on the front pages for weeks. He had to remain separated from the other jail inmates for his own safety. "Wanted" posters were circulated with his name and picture, and during the night deputies often overheard catcalls and threats directed at Crawford.

The search for Remington continued for a few weeks. On September 22, Sheriff Williams was quoted as saying there were still around forty investigators working on the case. The existence of Remington, according to Williams, "is the question of the hour." He said the force was about equally divided, with "half leaning one way and half leaning the other." There were a few leads to Remington's whereabouts, but none that proved worthwhile. Eventually, FBI investigators stated publicly that Remington was likely a fictional character created by Crawford to lessen his guilt and the search was ended, a fortunate circumstance for the man Crawford knew as R. L. Remington.

Curiously enough, representatives of the FBI revisited Crawford during his last years on death row, asking for more details about Remington. Their explanation was that other, similar kidnappings had occurred in Mississippi and Louisiana and they were interested in Remington as a possible suspect.

Part 8: Awaiting Trial

I

In jail, Crawford was perhaps freer than he had been on the outside. Circumstances were no longer within his control. His obligation gradually lessened, as it does when one is incapacitated. With loss of empowerment came release from responsibility, a new feeling for him. He had admitted to the kidnapping and was going to stand trail. There was nothing he could do, except leave his fate in the hands of others: attorney and family, the system, and what few friends were left. He began to feel what he first thought was despair. Later he recognized it as the early beginnings of a new inner peace.

Everyone knew. They knew about his debt, his failure, his weakness and his crime. There were no more secrets to keep. What more could they do to him? Bankruptcy? Loss of respect? What more could he lose? He was charged with first-degree murder. All that was left to take from him was life.

And Connie knew—that was important. He had wanted to tell her all along, about everything, the money problems, his feelings. He just hadn't been able, or the time wasn't right. Now that it was all out there, he felt closer to her. He wanted to talk to her every day. Local calls from the jail cost $1.55 and had to be made collect. There was a two-hour limit. Sometimes in the evenings one call wasn't enough. They would talk for two hours and, after the time expired, he would call again. He knew what time Connie came home for lunch, and he would call then. They talked about the family and about his case, but mostly they reminisced. They remembered the good times and the laughter.

For thirty-five years they had been deeply in love, and she stood by him still during his time in jail. (After the trial would be a different matter, but, for now, she was there.) And he felt closer to her than ever before—now they shared the burdens that before were his alone.

One matter of immediate concern was his choice of defense counsel. His first attorney, Adams, who was in his seventies and had not tried a criminal case in a number of years, both Crawford and his wife agreed, was not capable of handling a capital murder case. The advice provided by Adams immediately after the arrest had been either incorrect or misunderstood. Crawford later testified in pre-trial hearings that Adams did not warn him to remain silent and, in fact, encouraged him to aid officials in the search for McKay. Further, Crawford remained adamant that Adams had lied to him about having an agreement to prosecute the case in federal court instead of state court, because a death sentence was far less likely in a federal case. Of course, those early conferences came while Crawford suffered from sleep deprivation and felt an urgent need to purge himself of guilt. In such circumstances memory can play tricks. Nonetheless, in spite of Adams' competent work on their bankruptcy cases, they felt that, because of his advanced age and early miscommunications, he was not a good choice. But who would be?

There was also the problem of money—Crawford was broke. His sister contributed $10,000, and Connie said that, if it became necessary, she would sell their home in order to finance the remainder of the cost. Crawford understood the state's obligation to provide an attorney if he couldn't afford one, and he desperately wanted to manipulate the system into allowing Connie to keep their home and her teacher retirement benefits—the things she had worked to accumulate for thirty years, and because of him, she was now at risk of losing. Because of Texas' community property statutes, she owned half of all their assets, which, after the bankruptcy, amounted to only their homestead and her retirement fund. Further, since she had been accused of no crime, Crawford felt she would not be forced to liquidate unless both of them agreed to it and, although she was willing, he knew he would never consent. The issue of competent attorneys was unimportant compared with Connie's welfare—Crawford would have volunteered to give himself the lethal injection, bury the needle in his own arm, if he knew it would have protected Connie. These thoughts he kept to himself, sharing with Connie only the matter of choosing the lawyer who would defend him.

Legal fees, they knew, would only be a portion of the costs. In order for his defense to be on a level playing field with the prosecution, Crawford's team would need to hire their own investigators, expert witnesses, and all the other technical-support professionals to whom the state has ready access, but only those defendants with deep pockets can afford. There was no immediate solution—they would have to address each need as it arose. The first issue was to choose a competent and affordable attorney.

Houston attorney Mike Ramsey would probably have been Crawford's first choice. But, after reviewing Crawford's financial condition, Ramsey concluded that Crawford had no cash and insufficient tangible assets to afford his fees. However, he did recommend an associate, Cynthia McMurry. Ramsey promised behind-the-scenes help for McMurry and future legal assistance for Connie as well, should the need arise.

Meanwhile, Crawford was contacted by a hometown girl, who had once dated his brother and even babysat for his son, Chris, and later became a big-city lawyer. Her name was Wendi Akin. She had known Crawford and his family from the old days in Beaumont, and she knew that he could never have intended for McKay to be killed. She wanted the case, even offered to take it *pro bono*.

"I don't care about the money," she said. "I have enough. I just want the case. I'll be there for you whenever you need me and for as long as you need me. I know you too well. I know you couldn't have done this."

Crawford was convinced. He thought that because of her conviction that he did not intend for McKay to die, Wendi would now be the best to represent him. He shared these thoughts with Connie.

"Wendi . . . who?" She knew well who Wendi was. It was just that Connie remembered her as teenager and had no idea she had grown up to become a successful attorney. The thought of this fun-loving local girl in tight jeans defending her husband in a capital murder case was more than she could assimilate.

"I just don't know about Wendi. It'll be hard, coming up with the money, but I think you should go ahead and hire Ms. McMurry. She just seems so much more . . . *professional*."

Crawford was confused. He asked her to visit with both the lawyers before they made a decision. "I'll do whatever you want, just talk to them first. I've made so many bad decisions already, I don't trust my own judgment anymore."

Ultimately, Connie decided on Cynthia McMurry because Mike Ramsey had offered his assistance and because McMurry *looked* more professional. In the beginning, of course, there was no indication that she would quit the case just prior to trial.

McMurry became lead counsel and tried vigorously to defend her client, filing numerous motions, until May 20, two weeks before trial date, when she appeared before the court and asked to withdraw. The reasons she cited were a remark made by Judge Fred Edwards, and the failure of Crawford to pay any of the remaining $30,000 due on her contract. The remark by Judge Edwards occurred when he ruled that Attorney Rick Stover would continue as second chair at state expense in spite of the fact that Edwards had, during the same time period, ruled that Crawford was not indigent. This irony Edwards explained away by stating that his decision was "in the interest of justice," because McMurry, according to Edwards, "lacked the experience to try a capital case." Crawford thought perhaps she had overreacted, taking Edwards' comments in their literal context rather than accepting the more obvious intent of trying to ensure that justice was served while upholding the letter of the law. He also wondered if maybe she hadn't begun to feel that the case was not winnable.

The latter reason, that she had not been paid, was more substantial. It is a difficult decision for a judge to allow an attorney to leave on the eve of a capital murder trial, but to force her to stay and defend her client without being paid would definitely constitute a conflict of interest. Edwards allowed her to step down, appointing Rick Stover as lead attorney. Crawford, of course, had to agree to her release, but she had convinced him that it would be in his best interest. The court, she believed, might at last be convinced that he had no money if she withdrew for non-payment. If he were finally declared indigent, maybe, only maybe, the state would provide funds for the expert witnesses and testing needed for his defense. He consented to her resignation. And he regretted not allowing Wendi Akin to take his case.

II

Adjusting to life in the Montgomery County jail was difficult for Crawford. He had always been a survivor, but this was a circumstance he never thought he would be faced with. There was no radio or television. He was kept in isolation because of the threats to his life, the handmade *wanted dead or alive* posters found in other parts of the jail. His cell was seven steps in length, from end to end. He walked and turned, walked and turned, holding his rosary and reciting the 23rd Psalm. He exercised daily, doing as many as 400 jumping jacks and 120 sit-ups in a session. However, his telephone conversations with Connie were his primary source of comfort. He liked calling during her lunch hour, when he knew she was at home, making a sandwich or warming a bowl of soup. The jail employees on the day shift were often insensitive, refusing to roll the phone cart to his cell. But, when he caught them in a good mood, they would bring the phone to his cell door and pass the receiver through the same small door they used to pass him his food. He would reach out through the hole and punch in the numbers, waiting impatiently through each ring, knowing that before the next, he might hear Connie's voice.

Nighttime was easier, the guards were nicer. Crawford remembered Sergeant Pearce as the best. He was the only one who seemed to always remember that inmates were human, with lives and loves and feelings. He never compromised their dignity. He understood the importance of family and was never too busy to bring the phone so that Crawford could talk to his.

When Crawford wasn't pacing or exercising or talking to Connie, he wrote letters. He wrote to Connie almost every day. He wrote to his boys, his brother and sister, to friends, to ministers and priests. And he waited for the next court proceeding, when he would be taken, shackled in wrist and leg cuffs, to stand before the Judge.

III

The first judge Crawford faced was John Martin. Martin presided over the case until year-end, when Fred Edwards took over. Both judges presided over the 9th District Court; Edwards simply agreed to take over the criminal cases for a while, since Martin, scheduled to retire soon, was trying to clear his docket. On November 1, Crawford stood before Martin for the first of his indigency hearings. If he could be declared indigent, then the court would authorize funds to hire an investigator and other experts needed for research and testimony. It was round one in what would become a bitter finger-pointing contest between counsels, each seemingly more intent on winning personal battles than actually serving justice. Defense counsel Cynthia McMurry faced prosecutor Mike Aduddell—he was prepared, she was not.

McMurry came to the hearing with no hard factual evidence to substantiate Crawford's financial condition, depending only on the expert testimony of Mike Ramsey, who had investigated resources when the family had attempted to hire him. He testified that he had found that Crawford had insufficient funds to provide a defense. Logically, his testimony should have been enough, but in a court of law, evidence usually wins out over logic. Aduddell was able to produce financial statements from a previous year that showed the defendant to have a solid net worth. A CPA had prepared the statement, but what no one considered at the time was that the value figures were provided by Crawford himself, and he was no stranger to manipulating the value of assets. Further, the assets listed on the statement had already been encumbered in his recent bankruptcy filing and were no longer available to the court. Still, the statement was hard evidence and McMurry had none to contest it. The hearing on Crawford's indigence was postponed, and the court took up a motion to reduce his bond from $1,000,000 to an amount he might reasonably be able to provide.

Crawford felt the arguments and legal terms and lawyer gesticu-lations ringing about his head. He tried to pay strict attention and was able to at first, but the day was long, and he had placed his trust in McMurry—she was the one fighting, not him. But what he heard he understood, at least the way an ordinary person understands the right and the wrong of things. He heard the attorneys manipulating facts and figures, in the way he had long since learned, bending truth to suit their needs. He heard his attorney first argue that he was insol-vent and couldn't pay additional legal costs, while later in the day contending that his bond should be reduced to an amount he could afford. Aduddell, on the other hand, argued that he had money and the court shouldn't have to pay for any of his defense, and, only hours later, he heard the same attorney take the stance that, since he had no money to make even a lesser amount of bond, the judge should leave it set at $1,000,000. It was nothing more than a game, and none of this surprised him.

The next hearing came on December 7. This time McMurry was better prepared to argue the indigency issue, but was still outdone by Aduddell. The motion was again denied. McMurry offered a compromise. She offered to begin liquidation, including putting the Crawfords' home up for sale, with proceeds going to reimburse the state. Martin's response was that they did need to liquidate, but he had already ruled on the issue. In addition, McMurry stated that, although two and a half months had passed, she had not yet been able to begin the building of any substantial defense strategy because she had no funds to do testing and the D.A.'s office was not forthcoming with evidence they had collected. McMurry quoted Aduddell as saying he "would not be giving me anything." She further stated that he told her that she would have to "pull teeth to get anything out of the file." It seemed obvious that the prosecutor had taken a strong personal interest in the prosecution of this case.

Judge Martin did, however, in spite of the fact that he ruled that Crawford was not entitled to state funds for defense, make some considerations in the interest of justice. He had previously approved, at state expense, Rick Stover's appointment as second chair. Further, he authorized ballistics testing for the defense. The playing ground was still far from level, but it was a start.

IV

Christmas came sadly for Crawford. It was a holiday that was important to him, a time for families to be together and celebrate. He believed in the commercialized version of Christmas, the one with color and glamour and glitz, with lights and hanging tinsel. He wanted to give lavish presents and spread happiness and joy. He had not yet conceded that he had spent his last Christmas with his wife and sons, but he knew McKay's family would no longer be together—and he was at fault.

V

The next judge Crawford faced was Fred Edwards, a brilliant legal mind with an impressive resume. However, from the start Crawford thought he felt a personal disdain from Edwards. It was a feeling that grew as time passed, eventually convincing him that this judge in his case bore him an intense hatred.

Crawford felt, as did his attorneys, that it would probably have been impossible for anyone who lived in the Conroe area to see him without at least some inert bias. The local jury pool had been contaminated by all the publicity, the judge agreed. After hearing two days of testimony from area news sources, which included examples comparing Crawford with such noted villains as Lee Harvey Oswald and serial killer Henry Lee Lucas, Edwards granted a change of venue.

When contacted by a local newspaper for a statement, District Attorney Dan Rice remarked that Crawford's guilt would not change, no matter where the trial was held. "We think he's guilty in Conroe, and he's guilty in Bryan, and he's guilty in Oklahoma City." The quote led to a charge by defense counsel that Rice had violated a gag order earlier imposed. McMurry asked for sanctions against Rice, to which Edwards stated that, if considered at this time, it would distract him from the trial at hand. He indicated that the matter would be addressed after the trial had ended.

The question remaining for Edwards, and the one on which everyone was speculating, was where to hold the trial. Crawford's attorney hoped for El Paso, a city more than 700 miles away. Her reasoning was that, in addition to the distance factor, which would greatly lessen the chance of a pre-exposed jury pool, the large percentage of Catholics in the area would be an advantage to her client. The flaw in her logic was that no one wanted to see her client gain any kind of *advantage*.

For justice to be served, if it is indeed a contest, the playing field should be level. However, when the trial site was finally announced, any hopes for a level playing field were dashed. Edwards selected the nearby town of Huntsville, in Walker County, just thirty miles to the north. The irony in this selection is that Huntsville is, for the most part, in the same media pool as Conroe. Two primary employers in Huntsville are the massive state prison system, which, at the time, housed death row and still houses the execution chamber, and Sam

Houston State University, a college especially noted for its criminal justice department. (The trial itself was held on university grounds). Scores of Montgomery county residents work and attend college in and around Huntsville. It is generally considered to be a sister city to Conroe, with lives and businesses that overlap between each. Officially, it answered the defense request for a change of venue. Unofficially, however, it wasn't much different than moving to another site in the same county. Members of the prosecution team and most residents in general were pleased with the choice. Crawford would soon feel the sting of Texas justice.

During the same time frame, McMurry again requested a bond reduction for Crawford. Prosecutors protested, this time bringing in a witness, James Collin Gaffney, at the time a federal prisoner convicted of drug trafficking, who testified that Crawford, during two two-minute conversations at the Montgomery County jail, told him that he expected to be released on bond soon and planned to "lay low" afterward. The implication, as Gaffney interpreted it, was that Crawford intended to skip out on his bond.

Anyone who knew Crawford well would probably attest to this testimony as unbelievable. Even his enemies, the ones who really knew him, knew that he could never desert his family. In addition, FBI agents had already testified that Crawford had previously had ample opportunity to run if that was what he intended to do. Furthermore, Collin Gaffney was Colleen Hawthorne's brother, whom Crawford had earlier fired for theft. It seems likely that revenge may have been a motive, or perhaps Gaffney was trying to get a sentence reduction on his federal conviction. Whatever Gaffney's motive for lying, Crawford denied ever making such a statement.

The bond reduction McMurry sought did not come until mid-March, when it was lowered to $450,000. Customary procedure for bonding agencies is to post the full amount for a 10% fee, or in this case, $45,000. Assuming Crawford's family could even find an agency willing to post a bond that size, the $45,000 fee was still beyond their means.

In a further development that complicated matters even more for Crawford, federal charges for mail fraud were filed during the same week. These were related to the insurance scam Crawford pulled off with the help of his friend Billy Allen some three years earlier. He had convinced Connie to hide her jewelry in the trunk of her Cadillac when the maid came on Thursdays, then had Allen take the car while Connie was at work. Insurance paid for the jewelry as well as the car, netting Crawford more than $50,000. It was the second time he had collected on a theft claim for the same jewelry. The scheme came to light when agents searched Allen's storage units for evidence in McKay's murder. Connie's Cadillac was still there, stored in one of Allen's units.

The oddity of the federal charge was in its timing, the same week as his bond reduction. Crawford was already in jail facing trial for capital murder. Why now, especially considering that the vehicle was recovered six months earlier?

McMurry openly questioned the motive of the charge, stating, "Between the state and federal government, they are effectively suspending the 6th Amendment right to bail. This, I think, is the first indication that they are both working in conjunction with each other because they're afraid that Hilton Crawford may make a bond." The charge was later dropped.

Through April and half of May, McMurry continued her diligent attempt at defending the most hated man in the county. She filed motion after motion, including a motion for sanctions against Aduddell and even a motion for Judge Edwards to recuse himself.

The animosity between prosecution and defense attorneys had, at this time, grown to an embarrassing level. Attacks from each side seemed more personal than professional. McMurry's motion for sanctions was in reference to a motion filed by Aduddell in which he referred to the defense counsel in a demeaning manor, calling her "ineffective" and "inexperienced." Edwards responded by blasting both attorneys from the bench. He called Aduddell's references "unprofessional" and "immature." He went so far as to threaten jailing both attorneys. "Keep in mind that the court has a lot of power. Don't make me use it, because I'm not afraid to." He further stated that if they did not correct their behavior, they would be trying this case "from inside the Walker County jail." The barrage lasted for more than five minutes. McMurry's request for sanctions was then denied.

Her motion to have Edwards recuse himself was weak, based only on the fact that he had signed a search warrant for Crawford's vehicle. It was heard and ultimately denied.

VI

Crawford was committed to his own defense, but not in any sort of active way. He left most of the decision-making to his lawyers, believing that, in spite of the odds against him, he would eventually prevail. Life had taught him that he could overcome challenges—he would never admit defeat until the final bell sounded. Yet, as his trial date approached, even he began to feel pessimistic. When McMurry resigned from the case on May 20th, with jury selection scheduled to begin on June 3rd, Crawford knew any chance he had was greatly lessened—when a coach pulls out two weeks before a big game, you're gonna want to bet on the other team.

Rick Stover was appointed first chair, and Lynn Martin was drafted to assist him. Edwards postponed the trial until June 17, allowing two more weeks for preparation. Also, although he still did not declare Crawford indigent, he appointed a DNA expert, a forensic pathologist, and a psychologist to aid the defense. However, these expert witnesses were designated by the judge, rather than simply ordering that funds equivalent to their fees be allowed the defense in order to select their own experts. The appointments worried Crawford inasmuch as he had already begun to doubt Edwards' impartiality. Nonetheless, he now had experts on his team, if only in three fields. With less than a month until jury selection was to begin, motions to prepare, hearings to attend, and expert testimony to review, neither Stover nor Martin would get a full night's sleep during the next few weeks. Then began their ominous responsibility of defending a man facing the death penalty.

VII

Judge Fred Edwards is a true representative of the people and, according to his resume, "a generally all around good guy." A Texas native who is sometimes seen on his days off in well-worn boots and Stetson hat, he seems as if he might be as much at home on a cattle ranch as in a court of law. Since 1993, when he first became a Ninth District Court judge, he has consistently taken active rolls in the community. On occasion, he has even been known to sacrifice holiday time with his own family in order to help prepare and serve meals for the Salvation Army. He understands the makeup of his district and his role in providing justice. Trial proceedings in his courtroom are handled efficiently and somewhat sternly, as one might envision a school full of unruly boys being managed by a seasoned headmaster.

Early in Crawford's pre-trial proceedings, Edwards made it clear to attorneys on both sides that the trial would be held in an orderly and timely manner, no matter what. "Whether or not you have a conflict, this case is going forward. If you have to go somewhere else, we'll miss you, but we're going forward." In the next few weeks it became apparent that Edwards meant exactly what he said.

VIII

It was late May, and jury selection was set to begin June 17. Stover and Martin were deeply engrossed in trying to form a plan of defense that might save their client from the death penalty. But the evidence was overwhelming. Crawford had admitted to the kidnapping, already a capital offense whether or not it was proven that he had murdered McKay. He had drawn a map to the location of the body, even allowing two taped interviews explaining his role in the crime. It seemed a hopeless undertaking—to be done in too short time. But, to their credit, they were diligent in their efforts. In truth, maybe that was all that could be expected of anyone in their situation.

The most likely plan of action was to try and have some of the evidence, particularly the confessions, thrown out. Crawford remained adamant that his rights had been violated in a number of instances. The fact that he clearly understood his rights beforehand, due to his background in law enforcement, was not at issue. Our legal system, theoretically, must afford everyone the same rights. Crawford had seen many cases lost or overturned on mere technicalities, and he felt confident that there were enough discrepancies in his case to prevent a capital conviction. His lawyers weren't so sure, but it was the only game plan they had.

Among the best possibilities of accomplishing the desired result were the early denial by FBI agents of access to an attorney, inadequate representation by Adams, Crawford's first attorney, and the indirect coercion of the defendant through deprivation of sleep and the broad-casted appeals of Connie and the Everetts. Motions were filed, and witnesses were called to support the motions.

As to the denial of an attorney, Detective Ervin testified that he read Crawford his rights and that immediately afterward officers began to question him regarding the whereabouts of McKay. He said that fifteen minutes later he was allowed to make a phone call. That was when Crawford called his boss, Marvin Keller, in order to tell him he wouldn't be able to deliver paychecks. While Keller was on the phone Crawford told him he hadn't been allowed to call a lawyer and asked if Keller would contact one for him. Keller agreed. Ervin testified that he didn't know to whom the call was made or what was said, but that "he [Crawford] was allowed to use the phone."

In testimony at an earlier hearing in Judge Martin's court, Ervin had responded to the question of allowing Crawford access to an attorney in a slightly different way. "Well, he made a phone call and solicited one on the telephone and he was transported to the county jail."

Crawford's recollection was different. He remembered asking to call an attorney three or four times and being told "not right now" or that "he could call from the jail" and "we need to talk about McKay first." After his arrest Crawford had fainted during questioning and it is highly possible that his memory was inaccurate on this point. But it is also possible—and certainly understandable—that officers were more concerned about finding McKay than they were in seeing that the accused was provided his rights.

The defense questioned Sheriff Williams, Detective Ervin, and Agent Jones about Crawford's sleep deprivation and the blaring broadcast of televised pleas by Connie and the Everetts urging him to reveal McKay's whereabouts. Williams testified that Crawford likely was under suicide watch and state-mandated procedure was for an officer to see him move—ask for a wave or verbal response every thirty to forty-five minutes—but that he had no personal knowledge of the situation. In fact, no one who testified seemed to have any knowledge of whether he was or wasn't on suicide watch.

Neither did anyone seem to know about the broadcasted plea, who put the television in Crawford's cell, or who turned it on. However, Crawford certainly watched the televised interviews—they had a dramatic effect on him. He was already laden with guilt, and when he saw his wife's tearful appeal he knew he had to tell. It was the image of her he had seen in his dream the morning after the kidnapping. The look on her face, her sorrow and disgust, was the image he would carry to his grave. After his trial he never saw or spoke to his wife again.

Other testimony came from Cynthia McMurry, Crawford's previous attorney, and from Attorney Mike Ramsey. Both had interviewed Adams and been told that he had, in fact, received a commitment from a U.S. Attorney that the case would be prosecuted at the federal level. Adams told Ramsey that he didn't remember the federal attorney's name, but told McMurry it was Bill Jones.

On the stand, Agent Jones admitted talking to Adams, but not to guaranteeing that the case would be federally prosecuted. "I told Mr. Adams that this was a case that had dual jurisdiction and that there was a federal violation in my opinion, based on my experience, and that I would do everything that I could to present this case to federal prosecutors so it would be taken federally, but that I had no authority to do that." He further stated that he had contacted Assistant U.S. Attorney, Burt Issacs, on several occasions by phone and at least one occasion in person, in order to show him the evidence. "I felt this case should be prosecuted federally for a number of reasons, based on federal kidnapping laws . . . .." Agent Jones retired approximately three months after this case and, by the time he testified at Crawford's trial, listed his profession as music teacher.

Adams denied making any promises to Crawford and all motions to suppress the confessions were subsequently denied. Attorney Mike Ramsey probably unknowingly summed up defense problems when he replied to a query by Judge Edwards regarding Adams' testimony. "The provable facts are probably more important than what the true facts are. It's unfortunate to say, but *provable* gets to be more important than what the actual truth may be." The *actual* truth, Crawford had already admitted, was that he was guilty of kidnapping—all the rest was manipulation of that truth, on behalf of both teams, prosecution and defense.

Another possible defense was an insanity plea. The motion, however, was not filed before the May 28 deadline. In cases such as this, when motions are filed late, discretion is left to the judge; however, defense had no tangible evidence of insanity when the motion was filed, a week after deadline. Thus, Edwards was hesitant to allow it.

It would probably have been to no avail; it is unlikely that Crawford would have agreed. An insanity defense would almost certainly have included exposing his compulsive tendencies toward gambling. In spite of evidence to the contrary, he insisted until his death that he was not a compulsive gambler and, in fact, was an overall winner. *They were just luck—the losses—all just bad luck—just a turnaround—just needed to get out.*

Crawford faced the resignation of his attorney, each defeated motion, each new trial challenge with typical gambler's denial. *I can overcome this. It's only a temporary setback. It'll turn. My luck will change.*

Among the other pre-trial setbacks was a motion *in limine* (outside the jury's presence) by the prosecution to prohibit the mention by witnesses of the possible involvement in the crime of other parties, namely R. L. Remington. The rationale was that any testimony about Remington would be hearsay. Edwards ruled that the attorneys must confer with him before allowing the mention of a third party.

Crawford and his attorneys discussed this new development. It presented a difficult problem for the defense since Crawford insisted that Remington killed McKay. However, now there could be no testimony to expose his version of the events unless he took the stand. He wanted to testify. He had thought all along that he needed to tell his own story, that perhaps the jury would see the truth if it came from him. *Thoughtful and deliberate. Not blurted out in a sleepless, pathetic cry for absolution.* However, both Stover and Martin discouraged him. They convinced him that if he testified, the potential damage would be greater than anything he might gain.

"Somebody's got to present this to the jury, else how're they really gonna know. They'll see the tape and just think I'm blowin' smoke."

Stover offered a kind of compromise. "I think I can figure a way to get it into testimony anyway. I'll try." Crawford grudgingly yielded to his attorneys' judgment.

One additional pretrial motion, filed by the defense and denied by Edwards, seemed rather innocuous at the time, but could have actually had a later bearing on the trial. It was a request to enjoin the victim's family from showing emotion while sitting as spectators in the crowd. In its application, the request would have been next to impossible to enforce. Nonetheless, the logic of Stover's motion would become obvious on the trial's fourth day.

USA WEEKEND

What's Woody up to now? ..
Inside

● U.S. confronts Serb tanks **2A**
● No room for bomb relatives **5A**
● Lifeguard on Atlanta patrol **1B**

CHS basketball standout eams Darrel Childers Memorial Award **9A**

Conroe Courier

Montgomery County's daily newspaper

Trial of the century finally at hand

Crawford trial begins on Monday

By GEOFF DRUSHEL
Courier staff

When capital murder defendant Hilton L. Crawford goes on trial Monday in Huntsville, a community will be watching.

The abduction and brutal slaying of young Samuel McKay Everett last year made national news, but it was here the ghastly crime hit hardest – his closest to home.

Monday, in a spacious courtroom at the Criminal Justice Center on the campus of Sam Houston State University," the long-time Everett family friend known to the 12-year-old as "Uncle Hilty" will face his accusers, charged in the Sept. 12 abduction and slaying of the Peet Junior High 7th-grader.

McKAY EVERETT

Crawford, 57, a former Beaumont police officer, faces a possible death sentence if convicted of the charges by a jury of eight women and four men selected over a two-week period.

The trial, expected to last about a month, was moved to Huntsville because of extensive publicity surrounding the boy's abduction and death, and the arrest of a man as close to the family he was one of the very few young Everett would have unlocked and opened the door for when his parents were not home.

Everett was snatched from his affluent home north of the city around 9 p.m.

See TRIAL, Page 3A

Courier file photos

(Above) Carl Everett holds a press conference during the abduction of his son, McKay, last year while holding the football Hilton Crawford (below left)

signed "from: Uncle Hilty." (Right) Irene Flores talks with her attorney. Crawford goes on trial Monday in Huntsville for the abduction and slaying of McKay.

Chronology of a Tragedy

From staff reports

Based on the arrest warrant affidavit and information released through news conferences and announcements made by the FBI and the Montgomery County Sheriff's Department, here is a chronology of events in the Samuel McKay Everett case:

Thursday, Sept. 12
■ 10:15 p.m. - Carl Everett returns home to find his son is missing. Upon answering a ringing telephone, Everett is told by a woman that his son has been kidnapped and that he must pay $500,000. The woman says she will call back at 8 a.m. the next morning. Carl Everett then calls 911 to report the kidnapping.

Wednesday, Sept. 13
■ 4:30 a.m. - Hilton Lewis Crawford, a close enough friend of the Everett family to be known to McKay as "Uncle Hilty" checks into the Best Western motel in Beaumont. Local authorities and the FBI, meanwhile, launch an intensive investigation into the boy's apparent abduction.

Thursday, Sept. 14
■ Time unknown - Crawford tells FBI agents that he left Conroe and he neighbors find a yellow Lufkin on Tuesday at 8:10 ribbon around the p.m. on a trip that ended in mailbox of the Everett Beaumont Wednesday home last September morning at 1:30 a.m.

Friday, Sept. 15
■ Crawford is arrested at 7 a.m. at his Rivershire home and taken into custody for questioning. Hours later, he is charged with aggravated kidnapping.

Saturday, Sept. 16
■ 12:30 p.m. - Carl Everett holds a news conference in front of the Everett family home, where he issues an emotional plea for the return of his son. Everett directs part of his remarks to Crawford. Sheriff's Department of-

See CHRONOLOGY, Page 3A

Investigation complete on crash of DC-3 plane

By DAVID K. WINSTON
Courier staff

CUT AND SHOOT — The in-

line at the time of the accident.

Several law enforcement officers

Trade center may be last chance for some

By NICOLE PONDER
Courier staff

Lynette Fregin says she has done everything she can for her 18-year-old son. When he was a little boy, she "watched him like a hawk," but he still got into trou-

"We try to select placement the child would benefit the most from. The trade center

never referred to a residential facility, which is sometimes the last stop before prison.

Fregin, her son and his lawyer all say that such a referral is their last hope for Shawn.

"He doesn't want to go to jail," she said.

Part 9: The Trial

I

According to execution records provided by the State of Texas for the period of 1976, when the death penalty was reinstated, to 2006, sixteen people have been sentenced to death as a result of Montgomery County convictions, ranking it number twelve in total number of death sentences. In addition, according to latest census figures, Montgomery County ranks thirteenth in population—thus indicating that it is keeping pace or slightly ahead of most other counties in Texas.

II

Huntsville became home to a media circus on July 8, 1996, with focus on the George J. Beto Criminal Justice Center at Sam Houston State University. News trucks ringed the area, hoping to catch glimpses of the accused or the victim's family as they were ushered into the rather plain looking brick building housing the University CJ facility. Inside, security personnel checked purses and briefcases and guided spectators through airport-style metal detectors. There was cause for all the added security—rumors had surfaced about an assassination attempt on Hilton Crawford.

Paulette Everett testified first. She was subdued and articulate in explaining her and her husband's past relationship with the Crawfords and the events of September 12. She said that since she and Connie had taught together, they saw the Crawfords a couple of times each year, and that McKay loved Hilton because he often gave their son presents, like footballs and bubblegum. The only revelation in her testimony was how few times the Everetts had seen the Crawfords during McKay's lifetime. Because of the press coverage, most people seemed to be under the impression that the two families were much closer.

Following Paulette came Randy Bartlett, the Everetts' next-door neighbor. He verified the events that occurred the night of the kidnapping, but also related a prior incident with the alarm system in the Everett home. His testimony indicated that the occurrence had happened probably a year before the kidnapping and that the sheriff's department had been contacted because of a tripped alarm. A uniformed deputy had come to the house and McKay would not allow him inside. The statement was intended to discredit Crawford's story that McKay had opened the door for Remington. The defense had no rebuttal.

After the trial Crawford was asked to explain how Remington was able to convince McKay to open the door. "I can't say. All I know is he looked exactly like a policeman—he had a badge and everything. The only thing wrong was the color of his uniform—it was blue, instead of brown, like the Conroe police. He told me he was gonna say that Carl needed some papers for the Amway meeting. That's all I know. I saw him talking to McKay through the door and then the door opened and he motioned for me to pull in the driveway. That's when he grabbed McKay." Since Crawford did not take the stand, and the defense was not allowed to question anyone about the possible actions of another player, there was nothing to be done except allow the jury to assume that a twelve-year-old, home alone at night, had done exactly as he had been told and refused entry to a police officer.

Next came the testimony of Elizabeth Schaeffer, McKay's girl-friend and Crawford's next-door neighbor. She said that she had been on the phone with McKay when he left to answer the door and never came back. She testified that she heard no beeping noise, like an alarm system being turned off. "All I heard was him set down the phone and opening the door. That's all."

Elizabeth was another child that Crawford had known since birth. He had shown her the same attention and generosity he did most children. His driveway was next to the Schaffer house, and when Elizabeth saw him come in, she would often open her window and talk to him. He was patient and would always take time to visit with her. Sometimes she brought two or three plums from her tree and he ate them in front of her. "Ummmm." He would shake his head and make a face of delight. "Ummmm, soooo goood." And she would giggle. She testified that Mr. Crawford was a kind person, he was fun to be around, he liked kids, and Mrs. Crawford was a sweet lady.

The jury heard testimony from three more witnesses on the first day. Bill Kahn described the way the Chrysler pulled into and out of the Everett's driveway, almost backing into his garbage cans. Carl Everett told of coming home and finding McKay gone, of searching frantically for his son, and of the raspy-voiced ransom caller who demanded $500,000 in $100 bills. He also said that although it was unusual, he had come home before to find that McKay had left the door standing open. The last witness of the day was a 911 operations manager who testified as to the time of Everett's frantic call to say his son had been kidnapped.

For most of the following day, Tuesday, only law officers were called. Deputy Thomas Taylor was the officer who investigated the alarm activation in the summer of 1994, when McKay refused to open the door. He was called to support the previous testimony of Randy Bartlett.

After Bartlett came Bruce Zenor, one of the first deputies to answer the 911 call. He testified that the house was already full of friends and family when he arrived. He and his partner tried to cordon off the area as best they could, but he knew much of the evidence would already be tainted.

Next came Norbert LeBlanc, a Montgomery County crime-scene investigator specializing in fingerprints. He told of finding no unusual prints around the door from which McKay was abducted. He did, however, find shoe imprints in the hallway dust for which he was unable to find an owner. None of the ten pairs of shoes or two pairs of boots seized from Crawford's home matched the impressions. He further testified that Crawford's car, which he said had been recently detailed, contained only Crawford's prints.

Anthony Wargo, who managed the investigation at the Everett's home, was next in line. He described the scene as he arrived as confused, with people "milling around." He explained how he gained control as best he could and tried to deal with well-meaning neighbors as they offered help and consolation to their friends. He told how, with Carl's help, he compiled three lists: friends who McKay would have opened the door for, people who were scheduled to attend the Amway meeting, and friends who drove a car like the one Bill Kahn had seen. He related how Crawford appeared on all three lists, enabling them to focus their search. He told of ordering a "trap and trace" to be installed at the Everetts', and of staying awake for hours on end in the hope of finding young McKay still alive.

Next up was Christopher Charles Siffert, a fraud-control manager with Houston Cellular, Crawford's cell phone provider. Siffert, as well as the next two witnesses, also employees of Houston Cellular, explained how their trace equipment worked, how they could tell the approximate area from which a call was made, the duration of the call, and to what number a call was placed. It was this information that led agents to Irene Flores, the raspy-voiced caller who made the ransom demand.

The last three calls to Flores' number were all from the Lake Charles area, on the night of the kidnapping, at 11:10 for two minutes, again at 11:13 for three minutes, and finally at 11:30 for six minutes. The first of these three would have been when the kidnappers learned that Flores had not returned to her home after making the ransom call from a nearby pay phone. McKay's abductors had no way of knowing at the time, but Flores thought that after getting through to Carl Everett her role had been fulfilled—she then went to a neighborhood bar frequented by other gay and lesbian singles, where she drank, danced, and talked for the rest of the evening until the bar closed in the early morning hours. She gave no thought to the welfare of McKay—Crawford had told her it was just a scam, and she believed him.

The second call Crawford made was to make sure he had under-stood correctly—Flores' mother didn't speak English well—and to tell her that if Irene returned not to allow her to leave. He tried to impress on her the importance of this message. The Lake Charles area would have also been the approximate time and place Crawford remembered McKay becoming noisy in the trunk. Remington would have already been angry, and he became even more so.

The last call, the six-minute call at 11:30, was undoubtedly the most fateful one for McKay. This would have been the one during which Crawford tried to quiz her mother as to where Irene might have gone. It would have been the call during which Remington began to curse and yell, accusing Crawford of having "fucked this deal up from the start." It would also have been the one in which Flores' mother heard a man yelling in the background. She claimed the FBI never questioned her about the call. One possible reason is that they were too busy trying to prove their own theory—that Remington was a fictional character. It was probably after this call that Remington began to decide that they should cut their losses.

The next witness called was Ronald K. McCurley, a Huntsville-area supervisor who had worked under Crawford at Security Guard Services. McCauley testified that he had been scheduled to attend the Amway meeting with Crawford on the night of the kidnapping.

"I had talked to him—well, we actually talked to each other about going to an Amway meeting." McMurley stated that he was to meet Crawford at his home in order for them to go to the 8 p.m. meeting together. He was supposed to arrive early so they could get there on time. Unfortunately, and perhaps more fatefully than anyone could imagine, McCurley was late. He had planned to take a short afternoon nap and asked his father to wake him. However, he stated, "I guess I was too tired. I just went back to sleep." He woke the second time at around twenty or twenty-five minutes to eight. He drove as fast as he could, but he guessed he was still at least ten minutes late in getting to the Crawford residence. The house was dark. He rang the bell but no one answered.

In a later interview Crawford was asked what he would have done if McCurley had gotten there on time. He shrugged. "I guess I woulda gone to the meeting. I never really thought this kidnappin' thing was gonna happen. I kinda wanted it to because I needed the money, but at the same time, I didn't." McCurley also testified that he had known Crawford for more than three years. He said that Crawford was a "good guy" who "does his work."

Nancy Kahn, wife of Bill Kahn, came next. She substantiated her husband's earlier testimony regarding the time period during which he was putting out the garbage. She also testified about the frantic state of Carl and Paulette as they came to realize their son's plight. She told of Carl screaming out, in her home, "McKay's been kidnapped!" and of him hitting the wall with his fist. She also recounted the phone calls she got from the Crawfords. Connie Crawford called her around midnight and said that she would call Connie Schaeffer, the mother of McKay's girlfriend, and see if she had spoken to McKay. Ms. Schaeffer called the Kahn residence a half-hour later to relate the story of Elizabeth's phone conversation with McKay.

Mrs. Kahn also related how Hilton Crawford called her the next morning around 7:30, wanting to know what had happened, and if the police had any leads. This call would have been when she told him that the FBI was already on the case. It was made after he had given up trying to clean the blood from his trunk, and during the time that he was trying desperately to cover his tracks.

In addition, she told about a second call from Crawford at 2 p.m. By this time he was back in Conroe. He had already disposed of the bloody trunk liner and the gun, and he had begun to think that maybe he could pull off one final upset victory and make it out of the mess he had gotten himself into. He had already been interviewed by two female FBI agents, and they hadn't given him reason to think he was being singled out. The Crown emblem would be a problem, but he had found out in time to remove it. They might suspect, but if he just stayed on top of things . . . . As an afterthought, Crawford asked Mrs. Kahn to pass the Everetts a message: "Tell them I'm concerned and if there's anything I can do, please call me."

She also told of a third and final call that came at 5 p.m. By then Crawford had lost the momentary feeling of confidence he experienced earlier. Time had passed, and some of the people he had thought would lie for him were not sounding cooperative—he felt like a loser again, paranoid and desperate. He asked if she had relayed the message he had left earlier. She hadn't. "This is important," he told her. "Write this down so you can remember to tell Carl. Let him know I really want to help if there's any way I can." She testified that Crawford sounded a little strange to her, but the last several hours had been a strange time for everyone.

The last witness of the day, Marisa Pickering, pled her Fifth Amendment right not to testify on the grounds of self-incrimination. When Flores was interviewed after the trial, she said that Pickering was a friend of hers in whom she confided. She stated that the confidence was shared after the crime had happened and Pickering did not report the conversation because she didn't want to betray a friend. She said Pickering had no first-hand knowledge of the crime.

Wednesday, the following day of testimony, began with two

employees of the Best Western Motel in Beaumont testifying that Crawford had checked in during the early morning hours of September 13. The manager, Grace Wathen, verified the authenticity of motel reports that showed Hilton Crawford checking in at 4:37 a.m. and checking out at 7:23 a.m. Phone calls made from his room were a call to his wife at 6:35 a.m. and another to the Kahn residence at 7:24 a.m. Wathen explained that the time on the second call, showing that it was made one minute after checking out, would have been due to computer lag time.

Bambi Carter, the night auditor, remembered Crawford. Rather, she remembered his name and the fact that he was balding. When questioned by the FBI during the investigation, she was able to recall no other features. But Crawford remembered her well, her round eyes that seemed to burn with suspicion. He also recalled the way his hands shook when he tried to fill out the registration card and his sinking sensation when he noticed the blood spatters on his shirt. He didn't remember walking out of the lobby, but he remembered seeing the bloody rear car bumper in the lights of the motel canopy. He remembered, vaguely, the feeling of guilt as he desperately tried to clean the blood from inside the Chrysler's trunk before dawn broke and the whole world could see.

Next in line was Diane Allen, wife of Billy Allen. She recounted the telephone call from Crawford as he searched for Billy early Wednesday morning. She further testified that she had known Crawford for almost six years and had known about him even before that. She said that he had been a kind man to her and her family and she could not believe he had done something like this.

Billy Allen testified next. He recounted their meeting on the morning of the thirteenth and Crawford's wild story about an unlicensed security guard who had been wounded in a shootout while using Crawford's gun. He told of loaning his friend a screwdriver to remove the trunk liner and of hiding a garbage bag containing evidence, including the murder weapon. He described burning the bloody trunk carpet and accepting a bottle of champagne from Crawford. He also said that Hilton Crawford was probably his best friend, and he really did not want to be testifying at his trial.

The next two witnesses were FBI agents Roger Humphrey and Ralph Harp, who each in turn described recovering the evidence from

Allen and transporting it to the appropriate testing authorities. After them came Nick Fratta, with Alcohol, Tobacco and Firearms. He testified that the weapon was a .45 caliber Smith & Wesson automatic that was purchased by Hilton Crawford at Oshman's Sporting Goods. Nothing in the testimony of these three expert witnesses offered anything more than what Crawford had already admitted to in his taped confession.

Crawford's friend Gary Capo was next to take the stand. Capo told of knowing Crawford since 1969, when they were both officers with the Jefferson County Sheriff's Department. He described Crawford as a capable and well-respected Captain, who would have made a fine Sheriff. In fact, he believed in him so much that he had resigned in order to campaign in Crawford's 1975 race for sheriff. "Hilton and I became very good friends, and the only way I can describe it is—just very good friends."

"You cared a lot about Mr. Crawford?"

"Oh, yes."

Capo knew Billy Allen and had by chance been present on the morning of the thirteenth when Crawford arrived at Allen's storage lot. Capo was talking with Allen with his back to Crawford.

"When you turned around, you saw Mr. Crawford. What happened, if anything?"

"Well, he stopped. He just stopped dead in his tracks, just stood there, looking at me."

"What did you do?"

"Just stood there. I told him, I said, 'Come on over and say hello.' There's a slight ditch there and he stepped over it and started approaching me and Mr. Allen, but he never made eye contact with me. I put my hand out to shake hands with him and he put his hand down, but he wasn't looking at me. He was looking over my shoulder at Billy Allen, and he didn't even speak to me . . . . I could see something serious was going on . . . so I excused myself and left."

During the testimony, Crawford remembered what a good man Capo was and what a good friend he had been. *Shoulda stayed in touch with friends—the good ones—the ones that don't expect anything from you—maybe just talked to somebody—who knows?*

John Schaeffer, father of Elizabeth, came next. He told about waking his daughter up to ask if she had talked to McKay, and about the FBI who came to interview Elizabeth at 4:30 a.m. He said that Hilton had gotten home around 11 a.m. the following morning and that "he didn't quite seem himself, not as jovial as he usually was."

Schaeffer further testified that he had lived beside Crawford for fourteen years and that they had been good friends, had eaten in each other's homes, and the girls had often used the Crawfords' pool. Crawford had even loaned the Schaeffer family his new car for a vacation once, when they expressed concern about their car making the trip. He even, on occasion, loaned Schaeffer his custom golf clubs. Schaeffer summed up their fourteen-year relationship very simply: "Hilton was a good neighbor."

Next up was Pamela Trull, office manager for Crown Jeep Eagle Chrysler Plymouth, where Crawford's LHS had been purchased. Her testimony was simple. She stated that, according to their records, the Crawfords really did own the vehicle in question.

One of Crawford's employees then took the stand. Melvin L' Esperance explained how Crawford had called for his son, Billy Tankersly, also a Crawford employee, the day after the kidnapping. While waiting for Billy to come to the phone, Crawford mentioned that the night before, he had come by the Jasper plant, where Melvin worked, to leave some uniforms. L'Esperance testified that he thought it was odd since he hadn't seen Crawford or the uniforms. Crawford said if anyone asked why he was at the gate with his trunk open, it was "because he was delivering uniforms." L'Esperance said he handed the phone to Billy and remarked to his wife, "I didn't see no uniforms."

Tankersly took the stand next and said Crawford told him that a private investigator would be coming by claiming to be an FBI agent and that he should say that Crawford had been with him the night before. Tankersly at first did as he was asked. "I figured it was something to do with a woman." When Agent Myers showed his identification, and he realized the agents were legitimate, he told the whole story.

The last witness of the day was a representative of a local car dealership, who said that Crawford had called her on the day after the kidnapping to find the price on a new trunk liner and mat for his LHS. He told her the old one had been ruined when he accidentally opened the trunk during a rainstorm.

The following day began with the testimony of Gale Vohs, a

Security Guard Services supervisor who worked at the Louisiana Pacific plant in Lufkin, under Crawford's management. He said that Crawford had called him on the day after the kidnapping and had told him that he had visited the plant on Tuesday evening. He explained that Crawford had asked him to vouch for the fact that he had been there in case someone came around asking questions.

Vohs refused. "I don't doubt you were here, but I cannot verify it because I didn't see you." Crawford said he understood and asked for the number of the female guard on duty that night—he said he had spoken to her. Vohs gave him a telephone number for Karen Dominy.

Next came Rebecca Hanley, a civilian employee of the FBI, who testified to the chain of custody for a taped recording of a conversation between Crawford and Dominy, yet to be introduced into evidence.

Then came FBI Agent Glenn Martin, who engineered the recording. After learning that Crawford had asked Dominy to say he had visited the plant on Tuesday night, Martin went to Dominy's home and asked her permission to install a recording device on her phone. Afterward, Dominy was instructed to call Crawford and tell him the FBI was coming to talk to her and that she was nervous about what she should tell them.

Dominy followed Martin on the stand. Attorney Stover focused his cross-examination on the depth of instruction Martin had given Dominy before soliciting the call from Crawford. "Did the officer tell you what to say?"

"He just said to tell Mr. Crawford that the FBI was coming out to see me and that I was nervous. And I *was* nervous." Her last remark brought a flurry of laughter to the courtroom.

After questioning Dominy, Stover moved immediately for her testimony to be struck on grounds of entrapment: "Ms. Dominy and the FBI are the ones that got the call to be made. And, except for that, the conversation would not have taken place."

Edwards overruled the motion. However, its effect on the defense would have been negligible even if Dominy's testimony had been stricken. Her statement, as well as almost all the state's witnesses presented thus far, explained Crawford's actions as he desperately tried to establish an alibi and cover up his crime. Nothing, no witness or factual evidence, was introduced to dispute Crawford's version of the crime as related in his taped confession. In fact, the only probable effect on the jury was in demonstrating for them Crawford's devious actions during and immediately following the crime.

On the tape itself the jury heard Crawford attempting to convince Dominy that he had actually been at the plant on Tuesday. "Well, I may not have seen you, but I saw that other lady. I saw Stacy."

"Who is Stacy?" Aduddell asked.

"Stacy is Stacy Robertson, and it's a man."

Victoria Hale testified next and recounted her interviews with Crawford. During his cross-examination Stover, as directed by the motion *in limine*, approached the court to announce his intention to question her using the name R.L. Remington. Edwards cautioned Stover, advising him that if he asked a question like, "Did my client tell you R.L. Remington did something to this boy?" it would be a "self-serving statement" and not permitted by the court. He was then allowed to proceed.

"In connection with your duties in this case, did you ever talk to an individual named R.L. Remington?"

"No."

"Did you ever attempt to locate an individual named R. L. Remington?"

"No."

"Were you given that name by Mr. Crawford?'

"Yes."

Agent Hale's answers were succinct, as someone accustomed to being grilled by attorneys.

"When Mr. Crawford gave you the name of R.L. Remington, was that on the 15th?"

"Yes."

"What was his emotional state at that time?"

"I would say he was very . . . distraught."

Stover thanked her for her testimony. There was nothing more he could ask this witness about Remington that did not exceed the court-imposed boundary of eliciting a *self-serving* statement.

Crawford's employer and friend, Marvin Keller, was the next witness. Keller told of knowing Crawford since 1979 and of their working together for nine years. He also related what he knew of Crawford's financial difficulties.

Stover asked about Crawford's treatment of his employees.

"What would you say that his relationship with his guards was, as far as caring about them, looking after them?"

"He was good to his people."

"Was he concerned about getting them paid?"

"Oh, yes."

"Were you aware that after he sold State Security, he really got no money from them?"

"That's what he told me."

"And were you aware that . . . when he sold the company, the company kept the accounts and the employees; is that correct?"

"That's correct."

"And were you aware of the financial problems that were going on and [the problem of] getting the employees paid by the new owners?"

"Yes, Mr. Crawford went over that with me."

"What did he tell you about that?"

"He told me that they wasn't paying the people and he was having to pay them hisself. And when Mr. Crawford went to work for me and I took the accounts over, he even borrowed the money from me to pay off existing bills, some checks, then I picked up part of the checks for him."

"These were to pay off employees that weren't being paid by the new owners of the company?"

"That's correct."

Keller also confirmed that Crawford had physical problems for the last year or so prior to his crime. "He had blood pressure problems, he had stomach problems." He told of how Crawford would begin sweating profusely whenever an attack was imminent.

Next to testify were the owners and employees of Wilkins Cleaners, where police located the blood-spattered clothes Crawford had left to be cleaned. "The garments felt like, if you've been to the beach, they felt like a salt spray, like a sticky salt something on them," said Sylvia Friday, the employee who took the clothes in.

Under cross-examination, Ms. Friday testified to Crawford's demeanor: "He seemed tired. His eyes seemed very puffy, noncommunicative. He would not communicate. I try to talk to my customers. And he wasn't unpleasant, he just wasn't pleasant."

"Did he have dark circles under his eyes?"

"Yes, he did."

"Were his shoulders kind of droopy?"

"Yes, they were, and his eyes were very puffy."

After the four witnesses from Wilkins Cleaners testified, Agent Robert Lee of the FBI took the stand. Lee told of the interview he and Victoria Hale had conducted with Crawford at his office on September 14.

"When we first arrived to talk to him, he appeared to be very nervous. His hands were shaking. And he just appeared real nervous when we first got there." Lee said that Crawford seemed to compose himself as the interview progressed. He recounted the lies that Crawford had told as to his whereabouts during and immediately after the crime.

Agent Lloyd Dias was called next. Neither Lee nor Dias had any startling revelations concerning the crime. Their testimony was primarily to verify the chain of evidence and events: the stories Crawford had told them, and the evidence resulting from the search of Crawford's home and vehicle. It wasn't until Dias began a detailed explanation of marks found inside the Chrysler's trunk that his testimony became anything more than redundant.

Aduddell was asking the questions: "Agent Dias, do you notice anything unusual about the lip of the rim of the trunk itself?" He was referring to a picture of the trunk on the video imager.

"Yes, sir, the weather stripping located right here, when we opened the trunk, we noticed that it's depressed right here. The other side, you can see the difference between the two."

"It was different from the other side?"

"Yes, the other side is straight over here, where here, you have an indentation of the weather stripping."

"Does that indicate anything to you?"

"Yes, sir. It looks like something was pried in between the top of the trunk and the weather stripping to make it indent like that."

"Did it look like, appear to you that it had been done from inside of the vehicle."

"Yes, sir."

When prompted to identify a photograph, Dias explained: "It's a close-up of that same indentation of the weather stripping being pried downward, and it appeared that something was stuck in from inside the trunk in order to make it pried out like that."

"As if someone was attempting to get out?"

"Yes, sir."

As Martin rose to speak, a murmur had begun flowing through the courtroom.

"I would object to the prosecutor testifying as to speculating how or why those pry marks got there, like he just did, as if someone was trying to get out. I would ask that that be stricken from the record."

The hum became louder as Edwards reacted: "It's overruled. It's overruled."

At this moment, Paulette, McKay's mother, seemed to realize at once the desperation and fear her child must have felt in the hours just before his murder. She cried out, screamed with a voice so full of anguish that everyone in the courtroom was momentarily transfixed by the sound. They turned to watch. She screamed with a mother's rage, giving sound to the passion that had ripened with time and now had finally burst with red, running, pulsing anger.

As Judge Edwards ordered the courtroom cleared and struggled to regain control, Stover moved for a mistrial. "She has been screaming hysterically now for about three minutes in the presence of the jury. There is no way that this jury can give this defendant a fair trial after this exhibition."

"It's overruled and denied."

After a recess the jury was returned to the courtroom and Judge Edwards admonished them to disregard the outburst. Court was adjourned until the following day.

III

Judge Edwards began day five by reminding members of the gallery and press that they were to act in a manner "that brings respect and decorum to this proceeding." He recognized that "these are emotions that are present for both the victim and the defendant in this case," but he insisted on order. "We will behave. If we have problems, the court will be forced to have the persons removed and not allowed to return." From Crawford's point of view it was a little like threatening to close the barn door after the cows were out.

Agent Dias was recalled and allowed to finish his testimony about the indentations and pry marks from inside the trunk.

"They appeared to be fresh," he said, indicating that there was no rust or aging pattern to the marks. The assumption was clearly that McKay had tried to escape by prying his way out of the trunk. The attempt would likely have made noise that could have been heard from inside the passenger compartment. Perhaps these were the noises to which Remington reacted so angrily when he ordered Crawford to pull over.

Next called was Agent Kimberly Wilkins of the FBI. She told briefly of how she and Agent Taylor had interviewed Irene Flores at her place of work, the Houston Parks and Recreation Department on Lockwood Street. Flores took them to the phone booth from which she had made the ransom call.

"Did she voluntarily go with you and Agent Taylor?" Aduddell asked.

"Yes, she did."

"Where was the phone booth?"

"The actual address was 13642 West Mount Houston. It was in a strip shopping center." Wilkins told of retrieving the phone number and then taking Flores back to work. The purpose of her testimony was neither asked for nor offered.

Ike Cegielski, a crime scene investigator with the Montgomery County Sheriff's Office, was next to take the stand. He told of executing a search warrant at Crawford's residence, during which he retrieved a pager from over the visor in Connie's Cadillac and several cans of cleaner and solvent from the garage. The implication was that one of the solvents might have been used to remove the Crown emblem from the LHS. His testimony was, like most of the state's witnesses, redundant, since Crawford had already admitted to abducting McKay and using the LHS to do so.

During his cross-examination, Stover asked if Cegielski had checked the pager. "Did it have a live battery in it."

"I didn't check it."

"Did you check the pager to see what number it contained, if any?"

"No sir, I did not."

"Did you take any fingerprints from the pager?"

"No sir, I did not."

"So basically, what you're telling us, you picked up a pager, you don't know whether it was active or not, and you picked up four or five cans of common, ordinary car cleaning material?"

"That is correct, yes, sir."

Sheriff Guy Williams testified next. He told of coming to the jail on Saturday evening in order to offer Crawford another chance to talk. "I went over there to check on the jail, but also to extend to Hilton Crawford an opportunity to speak with me, if he had anything he wanted to say to me."

"Did you know Mr. Crawford?"

"I had met Mr. Crawford before, yes, sir."

"Do you know his wife, Connie Crawford?"

"Yes."

"How did you know his wife, Connie Crawford?"

"His wife was my son's, I believe, first-grade teacher."

"How old is your son."

"Fourteen now."

Williams' testimony revealed how closely intertwined the lives of small-town residents often are, offering even more reason for the abundance of emotion surrounding the crime and trial. He went on to tell of how Crawford had "hung his head for a second" and asked if he could call his wife and attorney. He told how he had waited for their arrival and how Connie had left her husband's cell in a very emotional state.

"She was very distraught, crying, or her makeup that she had on was running down her face. She was wringing her hands. She had a Kleenex in it. She was visibly upset." Williams had no way of knowing, but Crawford had just told his wife that McKay was dead, killed by his accomplice in the kidnapping.

He told how Attorney Adams had remained in the cell with Crawford for several minutes, how Adams had motioned to him and Agent Jones, calling them into a private meeting room, and how, as a result of the conversation with Adams, they had learned that McKay was dead and that Crawford was ready to make a statement.

Williams was asked to describe Crawford's demeanor.

"He was shaking real bad. His voice was cracking. It was a pretty emotional time for everyone in the room, especially for Agent Jones and I because we had worked so hard on that case."

He told how Crawford had tried to draw a map showing the

location of McKay's body, but his hands shook so badly that Jones had to take the pencil from him and draw the map himself, using Crawford's directions. And how, after they had the map, they relayed the information to Louisiana authorities, who, in turn, located the body and secured the crime scene.

Stover took over on cross-examination. "How long did your conversation with Mr. Crawford and Mr. Jones take place during this drawing of the map?"

"With just four of us in the interview room, that conversation probably lasted maybe, at the most, like about thirty minutes."

"In this conversation that you had with Mr. Crawford, he told you he did not shoot McKay, didn't he?"

Aduddell rose quickly. "I will object to that, Your Honor."

"Sustained."

Stover attempted to speak. "May we . . ."

Judge Edwards cut him short. "That is *sustained*. You were also instructed you were supposed to approach the bench." Edwards instructed the jury to disregard the question and ordered the attorneys to approach the bench.

"That is in total disregard of the motion *in limine*. You were supposed to approach the bench. What is your excuse for this?"

Stover attempted to justify the question. "Your Honor, the State went into this conversation. This is not something I offered. They offered this conversation."

Crawford noticed the color of Edwards' face—it was bright crimson. "Take the jury out right now."

Outside the presence of the jury, Edwards continued to berate Stover. "You are in direct violation of a motion *in limine* to approach the bench before any of these types of statements were brought before the jury. You are in direct violation of that order, and the State does not have the authority to waive this court's order, only I do. You do that again and I will put you in jail and hold you in contempt. Now, do you understand me?"

"Yes, sir."

From the defense table, Stover continued his argument for several minutes, until Edwards admonished him a second time and ordered the jury returned to the courtroom. Stover's effort to introduce the notion that someone other than Crawford had been the triggerman was quashed. Stover leaned in close to Crawford and whispered, "Well, I tried, Hilton. I tried."

Stover continued with his questioning of Sheriff Williams, which, because of the constraints, now amounted to little more than repeating facts stated under direct examination. Before he concluded, however, Stover asked to approach the bench once more.

"Judge, at this time I would like to go into the balance of the conversation that took place when the map was drawn."

"It's denied."

"May we have a bill of exception on that?"

"Make it after we adjourn today."

(Ironically, Edwards reversed his decision on Monday and allowed Stover to finish questioning Williams about the mention of R.L. Remington.)

The next two witnesses were Jerry Stassi and Marcus Guidry, both Louisiana law officers in separate parishes parallel to the Whiskey Bay area. They both had shared in the discovery of McKay's body.

The final witness was Stan Vogel, foreman of the grand jury that had examined Crawford's case. He was asked only one question of substance. Aduddell wanted to know if the members of the grand jury had used due diligence to determine the type of object used to strike McKay. Vogel stated that he didn't understand the question.

"Based on the presentation made by members of the District Attorney's Office of the 9th Judicial District Court, was the grand jury able to determine the type of blunt object, that particular type, be it a tire tool, baseball bat, I'm talking about the particular type of object, that could have been used or was used in the infliction of any injuries to the head of Samuel McKay Everett?"

"The specific type, no, sir."

The prosecutor likely knew the answer to this question before it was asked. If this is true, the only logic to the calling of this witness would be to let the jury go home for the weekend with the image of twelve-year-old McKay being struck with a blunt instrument—*a tire tool or a baseball bat.*

Stover had no questions for Vogel. Court was adjourned.

IV

On Monday the first issue addressed was the questioning of witnesses, in particular Sheriff Williams, regarding the participation of a third party in the crime. In response to a query from Judge Edwards, Aduddell stated that the prosecution "will have no objections to any questions Mr. Stover asks regarding the issue of any third party being involved in this, coming from either Guy Williams or any other law enforcement agent."

Williams was then recalled for cross-examination and testified that Crawford told him that he did not kill McKay, but that a man named R.L. Remington had actually committed the murder.

The next witness called was Blair Favaron, a Captain with the Iberville Parish Sheriff's Office, who directed the initial investigation of the crime scene where McKay's body was found. He told of the remoteness of the Whiskey Bay area and that bodies had been found there on prior occasions. He described roping the scene off and identified several crime scene photos taken at the early stages of the investigation.

Next he narrated, through question and answer, a ten-minute video indicating a drag path through the weeds to the body itself. McKay's corpse was crawling with insect larvae and had been partially eaten by scavengers. Aduddell provided the questions. "What are we looking at at this point?"

"The victim's head, right side."

Carl Everett, McKay's only parent present that day, was asked to leave the courtroom while the video was shown. From the jury could be heard suppressed sobs as the graphic footage played. Afterward, one female member was seen removing her glasses in order to wipe the tears from her eyes.

Favaron described for the jury how Dr. Freeman, the Iberville coroner, had performed a quick autopsy and declared that the cause of death was "a gunshot wound to the head." He also told how Kim Colomb, the investigator who had videoed the crime scene, had later found a hole in the body that she thought might have been significant and that there was additional trauma to the head. Freeman was called and returned to do a second autopsy. After reexamination, the cause of death was decided to be either a gunshot wound to the head or blunt-force trauma.

Favaron's testimony foretold of coming dissension between these two expert witnesses. Colomb continued to disagree with Freeman's findings, calling on Mary Manhein, a forensic anthropologist at Louisiana State University. Favaron said that, in response to Manhein's request, Colomb loaded McKay's disarticulated head into her station wagon and drove it to LSU, in Baton Rouge. Later testimony of Manhein and Colomb confirmed his statement.

To understand the dissension among forensic experts with years of experience, one must first understand that, unlike the popular *CSI* crime drama seen on television, much of forensic science is subjective—that is to say, largely guesswork based on individual theory and experience. Of course, some interpretations are more solidly based on fact than others. DNA evidence, for example, is said to be 99.99% accurate. For fingerprints, the accuracy grows dramatically as the number of matching points in an individual print increases. Originally, the term *forensic* signified debate. It has evolved to represent scientific study as applied to crime solving.

Conflicting testimony among these State's witnesses centered on the cause of death. Dr. Freeman, the coroner and the only witness trained as a forensic pathologist, was logically the most qualified of the three to distinguish cause of death. His finding, that a gunshot to the head or blunt force trauma could have contributed equally, came first. He also testified that the holes in McKay's body and shirt were likely made by an animal.

Colomb, however, believed the hole in the body was another gunshot wound, while Manhein said she saw no evidence of gunshot wounds whatsoever. Other investigators testified that two spent shell casings and one slug, all from Crawford's gun, were recovered at the scene. Thus, it is likely that two shots were fired at or into McKay.

Whether death was caused by one bullet, two bullets, or by blunt force trauma to the head, none of the scenarios offered would have completely disputed the version of events depicted in Crawford's taped confession. He said he heard Remington strike McKay twice when they pulled over after they began hearing noises from the trunk, and after arriving at Whiskey Bay, he saw Remington pull McKay from the trunk and fire two bullets into him. Whether Remington fired the rounds or, as the FBI believed, Crawford himself did, it seems unlikely that both shots would have missed at close range. With this in mind, Manhein's version was the least likely to be accurate.

Besides Freeman and Colomb, whose testimony came later in the day, the only other witnesses to testify on this, the sixth day of the guilt or innocence phase of Crawford's trial, were FBI agents who aided in the recovery of evidence at the crime scene.

The first tangible evidence to contradict Crawford's version of events came the following day. Buster "Butch" Emmons, a crime scene investigator with the Montgomery County Sheriff's Office, testified to the finding of blood spatter evidence underneath the top portion of the trunk, behind the lid. It was a part of the trunk that would have been very difficult to reach. Emmons had to lie on his back well inside the trunk in order to photograph the spatters. Emmons himself did not specialize in blood-spatter interpretation. His primary job was to collect the evidence. He determined the spatters to be medium-velocity, or caused by a blow from a fist or other form of blunt instrument. He also called the tiny spatters on Crawford's clothing medium-velocity.

H.G. Jerry Welch, with the Houston Police Homicide Department, who did have significant training in blood-spatter interpretation, was called in to help. He testified the following day.

"We look at a lot of different things, depending on what is available. We look for the size of blood drops, the location of the blood drops, sometimes it may not be blood drops, it might be a smear or wipe or transfer. We look for whatever pattern is there, the number of drops, how the drops could have gotten there, where it could have come from. This is the type of things we look for."

He went on to explain the criteria for determining different velocities. If you clap wet hands together, he said, the water would make a pattern representative of medium-velocity spatter. High-velocity spatter, he explained, is created when an object, usually a bullet, strikes at a very high rate of speed. The result he described as "more like a very fine spray." He also explained that the first strike would not cause spatter. The blood would have to pool first, so there would need to be at least two wounds.

On cross-examination, Stover questioned the validity of this type of analysis. "I gather that blood pattern analysis is a fairly subjective type of science. Is that correct?"

"Yes, sir."

"What you're stating is an opinion?"

"That is correct."

However, even if one assumed that blood pattern analysis is an exact science, Welch's explanation did not go far enough. Within each category he mentioned, both high and medium velocity, logic tells us there must be a range. If speed of impact is the sole criteria by which the pattern is analyzed, then there must be variations other than simply high-speed, medium-speed, or low-speed. When a human life is at stake, law officers should demonstrate a more precise analysis and what it means. Interpretation may lead juries to believe that they are viewing factual evidence. Further, if the defense team had ample preparation time and money to hire their own expert witnesses, it is very likely that the interpretive spin would have differed.

Crawford's account of what happened was that he was ordered to stop the car when Remington heard noises coming from the trunk. Crawford heard two heavy thumps, as if McKay had been beaten. This explains the spatters inside the trunk, but not the spatters on Crawford's clothing. The Crawford version is that after they parked the vehicles in the darkness of the swamp, Remington hauled McKay's body out of the trunk and laid it in the weeds beside the road. In the process, he noticed the zippered gun case that had been lying beside McKay's feet. According to Crawford, he was still under the impression that they would follow the original plan of transferring McKay to the Cadillac, then taking him to New Orleans. Remington removed the .45 and racked the slide, putting a bullet into the chamber as he walked the few steps to McKay. Crawford yelled and began to run toward them as he heard and felt the first blast. From instinct, he turned, and the force from the second blast hit his side and back.

Which version is the truth? If we are to accept Welch's version, that all the blood-spatter evidence is medium-velocity and, therefore, not caused by a gunshot, it would indicate that Crawford had beaten McKay. If this is the truth, *who* then fired the bullet or bullets into McKay? And where is the *high-velocity* evidence that should have accompanied that act? Almost any Texas son who has spent a portion of his youth plinking with a .22 rifle, firing at close range into the muddy shallows of a river bank, will tell you, after he has cleaned the muck and dirty water from his hands and face—*it's not all that scientific.*

would have had to lay their eggs beginning at daylight on the morning of the 13th. According to Dr. Meeks, that would place the time of death at sometime during the preceding night. In the end, after all the detailed explanation and graphic photographs, the time of death remained at sometime during the night of September 12.

Crawford's taped confessions were finally played for the jury on the afternoon of July 17, the next-to-last day of testimony. Jurors were provided transcripts of the videotapes so they could follow easily, but were told they could not take them into the jury room as they retired. They were instructed to leave them on their seats in the jury box. As preparations were being made for the tape to be played, Judge Edwards offered an attempt at humor: "All right. And so it's going to be all right for the court to leave during this three hours?" A spattering of laughter rolled over the courtroom.

Stover had tried many times to have the confession suppressed. Before the film was shown, he rose to object one last time. "Your Honor, we will renew the objection previously made."

"So noted."

The final witness of the day was Joe Duhon, Crawford's horse trainer. Aduddell questioned Duhon about an offhand remark made by Crawford that Duhon had repeated to Detective Kirk Ervin. The utterance had come while the trainer was trying to collect past-due fees amounting to around $4000. Crawford had simply stated that if he couldn't come up with the money, he would kill himself or someone else. It was a comment made in the heat of the conversation, meant simply to emphasize Crawford's determination to pay his bills, and Duhon understood it as such. His testimony obviously reflected his regret at mentioning it.

"Yes. That's a true statement to a certain extent, but I think it was an expression that maybe I might even make that because he owed me money. It was not a joke but, you know, I kind of made that I wanted my money." Duhon went on to testify that he wasn't even sure that Crawford had said it. "I don't know for sure if I didn't say it. I thought about it yesterday, I don't know if I said it or he said it, to be honest with you, you know."

Crawford heard Duhon's efforts to retract what he had earlier told investigators. *You're sorry for what you done. You're a real friend, Joe.*

But it don't matter none now. In later interviews Crawford was asked about the statement, and his friendship with Joe Duhon.

"Well, yeah. Joe's a good friend. But he's young, you know. He's got a little bit of a temper. I think I probably did say that one time when he was after me to pay him. But it wasn't like I knew then what I was gonna do—I wasn't even thinkin' about nothin'. I just wanted Joe to know he was goin' to get his money. I was gonna see to it."

Of the four people who testified before the prosecution rested on the following day, the only one of consequence was Seabie Herrin. Herrin came forward because some thought that he was the one who Crawford envisioned as a model for the sketch of Remington. In a heavy accent he told of knowing Crawford from the Houston racetrack. He said they had known each other well enough to talk at the track. He claimed that on one occasion, during the weeks just before the kidnapping, Crawford had approached him and asked if he "wanted to babysit a kid for a couple of weeks and make some money."

In later interviews, Crawford admitted to knowing Herrin only casually from the racetrack and denied any mention of offering Herrin the job of babysitting McKay. However, if Herrin *was* telling the truth, his account was testimony to the fact that Crawford *did not* intend to kill McKay.

On July 18, after calling in excess of seventy witnesses, the prosecution rested. Stover moved immediately for a directed verdict of not guilty, since, by virtue of his own witnesses, Aduddell had proven McKay's murder occurred in Louisiana rather than Texas. The motion was denied and court adjourned for the day.

The following morning Crawford was brought before the court. "Mr. Crawford, you have discussed with your counsel, Rick Stover, and your attorney, Lynn Martin, on numerous occasions over many, many days your desire to testify in this case. Is that correct?"

"Yes."

"And have you made a decision about whether or not you wish to testify?"

"Yes, I have."

"What is your decision?"

"I will not testify today."

His decision was made on the advice of his attorneys and was one he would later regret—not to avoid guilt or punishment—rather for the truth to be heard, in his own words, as he knew and remembered it.

During the proceedings Connie had not yet seen the inside of the courtroom. Prosecutors suspected she may have been complicit, inasmuch as having prior knowledge of the crime, but declined to subpoena her because they felt that if she were guilty, she would take the Fifth Amendment, and if she were innocent, she would only be an asset to the defense. Crawford always insisted that his wife never had any knowledge of the crime. He was equally insistent that Connie was not to testify—under any circumstances. He said that his actions had hurt her too much already. To bring her into the courtroom, in front of all the spectators and the cameras, would only mean more suffering for her. He wouldn't allow it.

Edwards gave his final instructions to the jury:

If you find beyond a reasonable doubt that R.L. Remington and Hilton Lewis Crawford entered into a conspiracy to kidnap Samuel McKay Everett, and pursuant thereof they did carry or attempt to carry out such conspiracy to kidnap Samuel McKay Everett on or about the 12th day of September, 1995, in Montgomery County, Texas, and in the course of kidnapping Samuel McKay Everett that R.L. Remington intentionally killed Samuel McKay Everett, then you will find the defendant, Hilton Lewis Crawford, guilty of capital murder.

The attorneys delivered their closing arguments, and the jury was sent out to begin deliberations. Crawford looked at his attorneys. Stover merely shook his head once.

Crawford felt like he already knew what the verdict would be. He needed to talk to Connie. He had called her the night before from his cell and she had been supportive, had told him she loved him, no matter what. He needed to hear it again—now. One of the jailers who helped transport him to and from his cell was sympathetic and loaned Crawford his cell phone. But the Connie he spoke to on this day wasn't the same person he had talked with the night before, nor was she the same Connie he had been married to for almost forty years.

The Connie he found on this day was cold to him, insensitive, she was more like the Connie he had seen in the dream he had the morning after the murder. In her voice he heard only disgust. "Hilton, I want nothing else to do with you. I want to get on with my life."

"But Connie, why? What's happened since last night?"

"Nothing has happened. If you truly love me, Hilton, the way you say you do, you'll respect my wishes. I want never to talk to you again."

There was only an empty buzzing sound where a moment ago her voice had been. He tried to call her back, but no one answered.

The jury returned, having deliberated for only an hour.

"All right. Mr. Crawford, please rise."

Crawford obeyed. He stood, feeling his legs might not hold.

"We, the jury, find the defendant, Hilton Lewis Crawford, guilty of capital murder."

He sat—relieved.

V

The trial's punishment phase began July 22nd. The State's most damaging witness was James Gaffney, the federal inmate who had earlier testified that Crawford had asked him for the name of his drug backer because he was looking to skip out and "lay low" for a while. Gaffney told an implausible story of a plot in which Crawford had attempted to hire him to kill Sam Petro, Crawford's business partner. Stover, in his closing arguments, called Gaffney "the most incredible witness I've ever heard in my life." He reminded the jury that it was Gaffney's sister who had embezzled enough from Crawford's security company to bring it to the brink of bankruptcy. He also pointed out that the State, with all their resources, had been unable to produce the check with which Gaffney claimed he had been paid. He urged the jury that they should find Gaffney's story "totally unbelievable." Nonetheless, there was no hard evidence to refute Gaffney's testimony, and it is likely that jury members, along with the others watching the trial, were looking for something that would tell them that Crawford was different—not simply one of their own who had committed this deliberate, heinous act.

Defense testimony was scheduled to begin on the 24th. Stover told his client it didn't look good. Crawford had given them a list of names, probably twenty or more, of people who knew him, who he thought would testify on his behalf. Of those, only a half-dozen or so had agreed to come forward. Stover pleaded with Crawford to ask his wife to testify. "Hilton, if Connie doesn't testify, you will get the death penalty."

"I can't help it. She's suffered too much already. I'm not gonna drag her into this."

The first witness to testify was Carrie Alexander, Crawford's aunt. Martin questioned her. "What type of son was Hilton."

"He was a wonderful son."

"Was he good to his parents as an adult?"

"Yes, he was. Very good."

"Was he obedient as a child?"

"Yes."

"Did he attend church?"

"Yes, he went to Robin Moore Presbyterian Church, and his daddy was an elder there."

"As an adult, did he contribute to the community or children in any way?'

"Yes, he was in charge of little league in Beaumont and in Nederland."

"How did Hilton feel about children?"

"He *loved* children."

She went on to tell about Crawford's dedication to his parents and how he cared for his mother during her bout with cancer.

Next was Aileen Graybile, a career teacher who had known the Crawfords and taught with Connie for fourteen years. Ironically, Ms. Graybile had done her practice teaching under Paulette Everett and had been McKay's first-grade teacher.

Martin continued on direct examination. "Did you learn anything negative about Hilton during the time that you knew him?"

"No, not at all."

"How did he treat his wife, Connie?"

"In my experience he put her on a pedestal. He kept her in this protective bubble. As far as her never paying the bills or never pumping her own gas in her car. He cleaned up the kitchen, cooked dinners."

"Was there an occasion when you had an opportunity with other teachers to discuss the cost of electric bills?"

"Yes."

"Did Connie even know what her electric bill was?"

"No. She said that she did not—she had not seen the bills in a long time. Hilton paid them all, and she didn't know what her electric bill was running."

Ms. Graybile went on to say that Crawford had never raised his voice in anger toward' Connie or his children.

Others appeared, each testifying to Crawford's kindness and generosity. They told of how nice he had been to them and what a wonderful parent he seemed to be.

His daughter-in-law, Susan Crawford, told about meeting him for the first time. "I had smashed Chris' car really bad, and I was really nervous and everything. I pulled up in the driveway and he met me at my car."

"Who are you talking about?"

"Mr. Crawford. And he came over. He said, 'Oh, you must be the lady that wrecked my son's car.' He had a big grin on his face."

Chris was the first of Crawford's sons to testify.

"Chris, your father has been convicted by this jury of a terrible crime. You're aware of that?"

"Yes, I am."

"Despite all that, you're still here to testify voluntarily?"

"Yes, I am."

"Describe to the jury, if you would, please, your relationship with your father as you were growing up."

"We had a very good relationship. He's always taken care of our family and given me everything I wanted any time I asked, and I've never had any problems my whole life growing up. Couldn't ask for a better father."

"Was your father a violent man?"

"No, sir, he wasn't. No."

"Did you ever see your dad lose his temper?"

"No, I did not."

Chris went on to testify about how his father pampered his family, shielding them from the normal burdens that most families share.

"Chris, based on everything you know about your father over all the years, is this action your father has been convicted of totally, completely out of character with the man that you've known since your birth?"

"Yes, it is."

"Are you asking this jury to spare your father's life?"

"Yes, I am."

Next came Kevin, Crawford's youngest son, who echoed feelings of patriarchal devotion expressed by his brother.

Stover continued his line of questioning, aimed at showing the jury Crawford's true nature. "When you were growing up, was your house open to all your friends?"

"Yes, definitely."

"Bunch of your friends that grew up with you . . . you've seen them here today, have you not?"

"Yes sir, well, more. Many more."

"How were all your friends treated by your father, specifically?"

"Graciously. He always at meals, opened his house, drinks, let them go swimming when we had a swimming pool, did everything for us."

"Describe the relationship between you and your father."

"It was real close. He took really good care of me."

"You love your father very much, don't you?"

"Yes, sir."

"How is the relationship between your father and your mother, Connie?"

"They were close, real close. He loved her and she loved him a lot."

"Was your dad good to your mother?"

"Very, very good."

"Did he spoil her?"

"He spoiled all of us."

"In all the time you were growing up, did you ever see your dad lose his temper at you or your brother or your mother?"

"No, sir."

"Did you ever see him exhibit any signs of violence toward you or your brother or your mother?"

"No, sir."

"Did you ever see him exhibit any types of losing his temper or being violent toward anyone?"

"No."

"When you were growing up?"

"No, never."

Kevin went on to verify that Crawford had indeed protected his family from any financial burden. True to his character, Crawford had told neither of his sons about the family's money problems.

The last witness to testify on Crawford's behalf was Walter Quijano, a psychologist designated by the court to assist the defense. Quijano seemed well qualified, having worked as a staff psychologist for both a federal correctional institution and the Texas Department of Criminal Justice.

Quijano testified that he had evaluated Crawford and found that his violent criminal act was a singular one driven by a very desperate need:

> There is no history of assaultiveness, violence, there is no—this is not a person with a violent and assaultive lifestyle. This offense was peculiar and atypical of him. There are histories of other financial foolishness but not assaultiveness. Given that 57 years of no documented history of violent assaultiveness, that is taking into consideration to distinguish from people who are chronically violent and assaultive.

Perhaps because of Quijano's accent, the jury did not hear, or fully understand, what he had to say about Crawford:

> The next factor is the pressure that must have pushed this typically nonviolent person into committing a very, very violent act. What is the pressure and is the pressure still present or is it gone? If it is gone, then the degree of dangerousness will, of course, be dropped. And finally, where do you expect this person to be in the future, where his dangerousness is being predicted. We predict, of course, he'll be in the prison, and in that setting, the probability of committing another violent act would be toward the lower end of the spectrum.

It is likely that the verbose quality of Quijano's testimony, combined with his accent, resulted in a jury effect that worked in opposition to defense goals. As to the key question of whether or not Crawford would remain a continuing threat to society, Quijano said: "My testimony is that in a continuum of very little dangerousness to very extreme dangerousness, he would be placed in the lower end of the spectrum, given the conditions that I have set." Had he instead, simply stated that, in his opinion, Crawford would not be considered a significant risk considering the fact that he would spend the rest of his life behind bars, maybe the jury would have taken his words to heart.

To rebut Quijano's testimony, prosecutors called Royce Smithey, an investigator with a little-known agency called the Special Prosecution Unit. Smithey explained, in a distinctly Texas drawl, that his agency was a prosecution assistance program that works off of a grant. "What we do is investigate and prosecute crimes that occur inside the prison system."

Smithey appeared unctuous, grossly overweight, and perspiring through a tightly tailored suit. But he spoke with a "Billy Bob" familiarity that jurors could more easily relate to. He testified to percentages and probabilities of crimes occurring within the prison system. He had no first-hand knowledge of the defendant, yet he spoke to the likelihood of violent crimes, such as the one that Crawford had committed, being repeated within the system, even referring to knowledge of aggravated kidnappings that happened on the inside. Under cross-examination by Ms. Martin, he was vague and uncertain, frequently using terms like "I don't remember" or "I don't know" or "I couldn't answer that." But he was always polite, always respected Martin's gender by responding with "No, ma'am" or "Yes, ma'am."

When asked how many cases he had investigated within the last year, Smithey responded: "Gosh, I'd say more than a hundred and less than a thousand. That's as close as I can get."

"So you don't know if you investigated one hundred or a thousand?"

"No ma'am, between one hundred and a thousand."

In Martin's relatively short cross-examination, Smithey addressed her as "ma'am" at least thirty-six times. His testimony never revealed direct knowledge of, or probabilities pertaining directly to, Crawford himself.

Before the attorneys delivered their final arguments, Stover had a final objection to the Court's Charge to the jury. The "Charge" is a deliverance to the jury, by the judge, of his detailed instructions explaining the factors to be considered and answered in order for the court to pronounce final punishment. Since Crawford had been convicted of capital murder, this judgment consisted of only two choices: death or life in prison. Stover requested that wording be added to inform the jury that, if Crawford's punishment was life in prison, his eligibility for parole would not occur until the year 2036, or roughly speaking, when Crawford was one hundred and six years old. The request was denied.

Within the Court's Charge were explanations of three "special issues" to be considered by jurors in capital cases. Each issue was read and explained by Edwards. The basics of these were as follows:

1. Do you find from the evidence, beyond a reasonable doubt, that there is a probability that the defendant, Hilton Lewis Crawford, would continue to commit criminal acts of violence that would constitute a threat to society?

2. Do you find from the evidence beyond a reasonable doubt that the defendant, Hilton Lewis Crawford, actually caused the death of the deceased, Samuel McKay Everett, or did not actually cause the death, but intended to kill the deceased, Samuel McKay Everett, or another or anticipated that human life would be taken?

The first two conditions must be answered with a yes, unanimously, before proceeding to the third. Number three requires only ten *yes* answers, but twelve *no* answers.

3. Do you find from the evidence, taking into consideration all the evidence, including the circumstances of the offense, the defendant's character and background and the personal, moral culpability of the defendant, that there is sufficient mitigating circumstances to warrant that a sentence of life imprisonment rather than a death sentence be imposed?

After the Court's Charge, the attorneys were allowed to present their final statements, with Aduddell scheduled last. Emotions ran high as each of them offered their individual perspectives. Assistant District Attorney Neff began by using an extended metaphor related to *Jack the Giant Killer*, an old-time horror film where the monsters dwelled within normal-looking people and operated under the guise of kindness.

"They went around in the midst of ordinary folk like you and me." Hilton Crawford was her monster. "He looks like an ordinary, kind, normal man. All of his friends thought that. All of his neighbors thought that. All of his family thought that. Thought he was a good, kind, caring person." Neff told how McKay had loved and trusted Crawford, and how *her* monster had then coldly plotted and carried out the kidnapping. She emphasized the betrayal and the fear and horrible death McKay must have suffered at the hands of this man he trusted. Her delivery was focused directly at her twelve-person audience, leading them to feel the same distrust, the same insane fracture of morality that swallowed the innocent McKay—the same circumstance that could happen to them—or someone they love.

To emphasize her points Ms. Neff used a large drawing tablet propped on an easel and pointed toward the jury. As she spoke, she wrote one- or two-word phrases in large red marking ink, turning the pages as each was filled. As she approached her summation she said, "Hilton Crawford showed McKay no mercy," and wrote "NO MERCY." With her remark "he showed McKay no leniency" she wrote "NO LENIENCY." Her voice rose as she stated, "He imposed and carried out a death sentence on young McKay Everett." With a vigorous flourish she turned and wrote the words, "DEATH SENTENCE." She made no effort to turn the page when her state-ment ended.

Martin was next. Her oratory was inspired by the Bible, "our standard of behavior." She discussed the Ten Commandments and recited the Beatitudes: "Blessed are the gentle for they shall inherit the earth; blessed are those who hunger and thirst for righteousness, for they will be fulfilled; blessed are the merciful, for they are shown mercy." Her plea was based on a turn-the-other-cheek philosophy, not one with which people who had been shown the body of McKay Everett, crawling with more than a million maggots, could easily sympathize.

Stover was up next. He recited the facts of the case, rightly describing the crime as a "rash, stupid, out-of-character act for a desperate man." He pointed out that Crawford, a trained law officer, had left a trail that "even my old blind Basset hound could have followed." He covered each of the special issues cited by Edwards and gave reasonable arguments relating to each of them. His statement was centered in logic, but in his voice was a tone of reticence. There was no fire, nothing to convince the jury that he believed his own words. In the end he turned to Crawford, as if he already sensed the jury's vote. "Hilton, I've done the best that I know how." Crawford shook Stover's hand and patted his shoulder. Both Martin and Stover's oratories had been delivered standing beside the words Neff had written: "NO MERCY—NO LENIENCY—DEATH SENTENCE."

Aduddell delivered his address with a fury worthy of an old-time gospel minister, preaching in the fire and brimstone voice of a man who knows he is right. To the testimony of Dr. Quijano, who had said that Crawford's crime was a singular event and unlikely to reoccur in spite of its violence, he remarked: "Hogwash. Absolutely hogwash. Absolute. It astounds me that a man as esteemed as Dr. Quijano would come in here and try to run that up the flagpole and make it stick." He, in turn, refuted the statements of Stover and Martin, with argument steeped in emotion. He showed jurors their responsibility:

> I submit to you that the evidence screams just as loud as that little boy screamed in the back of that trunk, for yes, yes, no, for every right you cherish you have a duty you must fulfill. For every hope that you entertain, you have a task that you must perform. For every good that you wish to preserve, you will have to sacrifice your comfort and ease.

His argument was convincing. He told the jury what they had to do. They voted unanimously and the court pronounced sentence.

In the days that followed, Crawford's attorneys filed another motion to have him declared indigent so that an appeals attorney could be designated. This time the motion was approved, and Peter C. Speers III was appointed to represent Crawford in his appeals.

VI

For his seven-year stint on Texas' death row, Crawford was a model prisoner. Freed from the self-imposed pressures of his outside life, his health improved and he re-dedicated himself to Christ. There was seldom a time in which he could speak of McKay or the hurt he had caused without tears. He never saw or spoke to Connie again, but his love for her and his boys never lessened. During his incarceration prisoners on the row became something like a surrogate family for Crawford. His fellow inmates, the murderers and rapists who so brutally executed their victims, took the place of the children he had coached. No matter their crime, he accepted each of them. He listened when they wanted to talk, offering advice or words of solace whenever needed. The week before his death, he used his last commissary spend to buy two pints of ice cream for each of his fellow deathwatch inmates. And, in the end, in his final statement, he thanked God for his time spent on Death Row.

On July 2nd, 2003, Hilton Lewis Crawford was executed by the state of Texas. It was done with deliberate efficiency, like turning out the light as we leave.

Crawford's Final Statement from the Death Chamber

First of all, I would like to ask Sister Teresa to send Connie a yellow rose. I want to thank the Lord, Jesus Christ, for the years I have spent on death row. They have been a blessing in my life. I have had the opportunity to serve Jesus Christ, and I am thankful for the opportunity. I would like to thank Father Walsh for having become a Franciscan, and all the people all over the world who have become my friends. It has been a wonderful experience in my life. I would like to thank Chaplain Lopez, and my witnesses for giving me their support and love. I would like to thank the Nuns in England for their support. I want to tell my sons I love them; I have always loved them—they were my greatest gift from God. I want to tell my witnesses, Tannie, Rebecca, Al, Leo, and Dr. Blackwell that I love all of you and I am thankful for your support. I want to ask Paulette for forgiveness from your heart. One day, I hope you will. It is a tragedy for my family and your family. I am sorry. My special angel, I love you. And I love you, Connie. May God pass me over to the Kindom's shore softly and gently. I am ready.